DAUGHTERS
of EVE

To Aaron Freeman and Herman Feifel — L. H. R.
To my parents — K. T.

Barefoot Books
PO Box 95
Kingswood
Bristol
BS30 5BH

First published in Great Britain in 2000 by Barefoot Books Ltd
All rights reserved. No part of this book may be reproduced in any form
or by any means, electronic or mechanical, including photocopying,
recording or by any information storage and retrieval system,
without permission in writing from the publisher

This book has been printed on 100% acid-free paper
The illustrations were created from collaged paper,
blotted or painted with acrylic paint

Graphic design by Jennie Hoare, Bradford on Avon
This book was typeset in Hiroshige Book 11pt
Colour separation by Unifoto, Cape Town
Printed in Hong Kong by South China Printing Co. (1988) Ltd

ISBN 1 902283 67 8

British Cataloguing-in-Publication Data:
a catalogue record for this book is available from the Britis

1 3 5 7 9 8 6 4 2

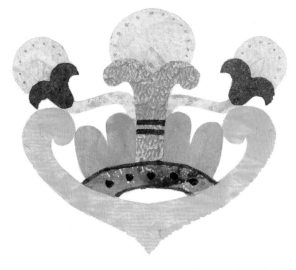

DAUGHTERS
of EVE

STRONG WOMEN of the BIBLE

•

written by
LILLIAN HAMMER ROSS
illustrated by
KYRA TEIS

walk
the way of wonder...
Barefoot Books

CONTENTS

INTRODUCTION

Three major modern religions, Judaism, Christianity and Islam, trace their roots to the Bible. The Bible is a 3,500-year-old library of Hebrew documents, and includes myths and legends, poetry, proverbs, songs, folktales and narratives. In particular, the Bible contains the laws and history of the ancient Jews, a people of spiritual sensitivity who believed in one God for all.

Because much of the Bible is written about men, I felt a need to discover the women who also made a mark on our way of life. What role did those ancient women play? Did they speak out or were they quiet in their strength? Did the women of biblical times dare to express themselves fully? And if they did, what was the outcome?

The stories you will find in *Daughters of Eve* are tales I have written after exploring the Bible and the Talmud. The Talmud is a collection of ancient rabbinical writings, written in the third to fifth century BC, that make up the basis of religious authority in Judaism. Talmud comes from the Hebrew word, 'lamad', to learn. In the following tales, you will find eleven descendants of Eve. Miriam, Zipporah, the five daughters of Zelophehad, Ruth, Abigail, Huldah and Esther are all biblical heroines. The Bible, in fact, makes few references to these women. For example, Miriam is mentioned by name only twice in the Book of Exodus.

A considerable wealth of literature can also be found in rabbinical commentaries known as the Midrash. The purpose of the Midrash was to penetrate the spirit of the scripture, producing an interpretation of the Bible which was not immediately obvious.

In the spirit of the Midrash, I have examined these descendants of Eve. They were not mere observers of biblical events, not just actors playing a role to further a storyline, rather they were living human beings filled with thoughts and emotions. My quest was to imagine the feelings and actions of the women presented here. In order to bring these women to life, I have used my pen to paint feeling, caring, questioning people whose emotions are similar to someone living in the twenty-first century.

Lillian Hammer Ross

THE JEWS IN EGYPT

*I*n Africa, a mighty river called the Nile flows north to the
Mediterranean Sea. Each year it floods, leaving behind a deposit of rich
earth. Thousands of years ago, the ancient Egyptians created a civilisation
based on farming along these fertile banks. The Egyptian kings, who were
called Pharaohs, also built massive tombs for themselves and their families.
About 2,500 years before Jesus Christ was born, they built
the Step Pyramid and the three great pyramids at Giza.

~

In about 1700 BC, the Egyptians were invaded from the north by the Hyksos,
who overran Egypt. They put their own leaders on the throne as Pharaohs.
The story of the Jews in Egypt began during the rule of the Hyksos when Joseph
brought his eleven brothers and his father, Jacob, to live there. They were
welcomed by the Pharaohs, and the twelve tribes of Israel were descended
from the children of Joseph and his brothers.

~

Then, in about 1570 BC, the native Egyptians overthrew their Hyksos rulers and
restored their own Pharaoh to the throne. This Pharaoh saw how many Jews
there now were living in Egypt and he was afraid that they might become too
powerful, so he tried to control them by making them slaves.

~

For the Egyptians, the new era was a time of great riches; the discovery of the
tomb of King Tutankhamen and its treasures shows us how prosperous the new
empire was, and how skilful its craftsmen were. It was quite a different story for
the Jews, for they were made to work as slaves, building the great Temple
of Karnak and the cities of Pithom and Rameses.

~

It was during this time, over three thousand years ago, that a little Jewish
girl called Miriam played her part in the history of her people,
and she has been remembered for it ever since.

MIRIAM

A cruel Pharaoh ruled in ancient Egypt. The children of Israel were his slaves and they worked for him from daybreak until nightfall. They made the bricks which the Egyptians used to build their cities. Pharaoh and his taskmasters treated the Israelites badly, but they could not break their spirit.

During this time, Amram, a man of the Hebrew tribe of Levi, married Yocheved, a woman also of the house of Levi. He was a labourer and she was a midwife. A daughter was born to the young couple, and they named her Miriam. In the Hebrew language, her name meant 'bitterness'. As she grew, Miriam came to dislike her name and she vowed that somehow she would save her people from this cruel Pharaoh. When she was three years old her brother, Aaron, was born. Both Miriam and Aaron would play an important part in their people's destiny.

Now, Pharaoh had astrologers whom he consulted constantly, and one day they came to him. 'O mighty Pharaoh, the stars have sent a message. A male child will be born to the Israelites. The stars have shown us that this boy will grow up to lead the Israelites to freedom.'

'What are you saying?' shouted Pharaoh. 'The Israelites are my slaves. They are not free.' He pulled at his beard. 'You speak of a child. Who is this child?'

'We do not know exactly who he is, Your Majesty. The stars have only told us it will be a baby boy.'

'Then we shall throw every baby boy born to the Children of Israel into the River Nile to drown.' Pharaoh stood with his fist raised high. 'I so proclaim!'

When Yocheved became pregnant for the third time, she was very frightened. What would happen to her baby if it was a boy? Then one night, Miriam had a dream. When she awoke, she ran to her parents to tell them. 'A very old man, dressed in white robes, approached me. He told me that the baby would be a boy. We need not fear for him,' she said. 'We must make him a basket like an ark out of bulrushes and let him float on the Nile. He will be safe in it.'

Yocheved held her daughter tenderly. 'You have sweet dreams, dear Miriam. We can only pray your dream will come true.'

Yocheved did not want Pharaoh's soldiers to discover that she was having a baby, so she stayed in her home and did not venture out of doors. And so, when her time came to give birth, it was Miriam who was her mother's midwife. Yocheved laughed when the baby pushed himself out with ease and the entire room was flooded with light. Miriam held her new brother, knowing that part of her dream had come true.

When the baby was three months old, Yocheved built an ark of bulrushes. She cried as she padded the inside with sweet-smelling cushions and spread tar on the outside to keep out the waters of the Nile. She wrapped the baby securely, laid him on a soft pillow, and placed the ark at the river's edge. Yocheved's heart was breaking. She was afraid that either Pharaoh's soldiers would kill her baby, or he would drown in the river. She looked towards the heavens. 'O my Lord, protect this babe.'

Miriam was worried about the strength of the ark, so she hid and watched it float away. It was summer, and the air was heavy with heat. Bithiah, the Pharaoh's daughter, came down to the waters of the Nile to bathe and cool herself. Her maids-in-waiting stood aside while she entered the water.

Bithiah saw the ark floating on the water. 'What is that?' she called to one of her servants.

The maid-in-waiting pulled the ark from the water. 'Your Royal Highness, there is a baby in it.'

Bithiah lifted out the crying child. 'Look how well he is cared for. He has soft cushions to lie on and he has been carefully wrapped. This must be a Hebrew baby boy. My father ordered them all to be thrown into the Nile to drown. This baby was put into the river, but in an ark so that he would be safe.'

When Miriam saw that the Pharaoh's daughter had found the ark, she stepped from her hiding place and slowly walked towards the princess.

The handmaidens gathered round to protect Bithiah, for strangers did not usually approach the Egyptian royal family. But Bithiah waved them away. She guessed that this girl must be related to the baby.

'Your Royal Highness...' said Miriam, bowing low.

'Yes, child?' Bithiah smiled. 'Are you worried about this baby?'

'Yes, Your Royal Highness. I know of a woman who would be able to nurse this baby for you.'

'Ah, yes,' Bithiah said. 'Go and bring this woman to me.'

Miriam raced home. 'Mother, Mother, come quickly! The Pharaoh's daughter has found our baby, and she wants you to nurse him!' Hand in hand, Yocheved and Miriam ran back to the water's edge.

Bithiah beckoned to them to come near her. 'I found this baby in the bulrushes,' she smiled. 'I will name him Moses, for that means "he was drawn out of the water".'

Yocheved and Miriam nodded and stood waiting.

'If you nurse this baby for me, I will pay you,' Bithiah said to Yocheved. She turned to Miriam. 'You must bring baby Moses to me every day so that I may watch him grow and he will learn to think of me as his mother.'

Every day, Miriam carried Moses from her mother to the Pharaoh's palace. She waited while Bithiah played with him, and then she carried him home again to be nursed by Yocheved. As she walked, Miriam held Moses close, sang him songs and whispered stories of their people's belief in one God. She told him tales of the Israelites, and recited the history of their time in Egypt.

When Moses was two years old, Bithiah welcomed him into the palace and she adopted him as her son.

Miriam was heartsick and lonely. She missed her baby brother, for they had been so close these past years. Yocheved was worried about Miriam. One day, she bought a tambourine in the market place. That night, she gave it to Miriam. 'Perhaps this tambourine will help you shake away your loneliness,' she said.

Miriam held the tambourine. Its tiny bells were silent. She raised it and shook it. It was as though the tambourine spoke to her, sang to her. Miriam laughed and clapped it again.

'Why not go out and show your gift to your friends?' Yocheved said, and soon Miriam was dancing with her friends, singing to the music of her tambourine.

Often, Miriam took her friends close to the Pharaoh's palace, hoping to catch a glimpse of her brother. On summer days, they hid in the bulrushes by the Nile and Miriam would tell and retell how Moses was saved by the Egyptian princess, but she did not see her brother again.

The years passed and Moses grew up. One day, news came to his family that Moses had killed an Egyptian. In fear of his life, he had run away. Miriam was grief-stricken. Where would he run? Where had he gone?

THE LAND OF MIDIAN

The Egyptian Pharaohs created a powerful nation and erected splendid monuments and temples in their cities. Their armies swept all others before them. In contrast, the people known as the Midianites were not a strong military or economic force. They lived on land no one else wanted, land which was too dry to grow crops.

~

At the time that Moses fled from Egypt and sought refuge with Jethro, the High Priest, the land of Midian was probably in the area now known as the Sinai Desert. Here the people followed the nomadic life of the shepherd, moving their flocks of sheep and goats from one green oasis to the next.

~

Unlike the Jewish slaves of the Pharaoh, however, the Midianites were a free people, but they always kept a wary eye on the Egyptians, in case they should decide to invade them. In an ironic twist of history, however, the strong, free Midianites were destined to disappear as a nation, and it was the enslaved Jews who carried their faith and retained their heritage throughout the ages.

~

Despite this, the Midianites gave much to the Jewish people. If you look ahead in the Bible, you will find that, after the Exodus from Egypt, Jethro visited Moses at the Mountain of God (Mount Sinai). Jethro saw that Moses judged the people's problems from morning to night, and he suggested that able men should be taught the laws so that they could become Moses's assistants and help judge the people. After this, only the most difficult arguments were brought to Moses and his assistants judged all small matters. Thus it was Jethro, the High Priest of Midian, who founded the Hebrew Judiciary system, in which the delegation of responsibility is as important today as it was in the time of Moses.

~

This story tells how Jethro met Moses for the first time, and how Jethro's eldest daughter, Zipporah, became Moses's wife.

ZIPPORAH

Zipporah, Gudit and Tanna, the three eldest of the seven daughters of Jethro, priest of Midian, sat in the shade of an olive tree. They were all three beautiful, with straight young bodies, shining dark eyes and full, smiling lips.

'What are you dreaming of, Gudit?' asked Zipporah.

'I no longer dream,' replied Gudit. 'Mother says that dreaming is a waste of time. She says that Father will soon choose my husband.' She played with the fringe on her dress. 'Instead of dreaming, it would be better to learn to weave fine cloth, sew a straight seam and to allow our father to decide our futures for us.'

Zipporah turned to Tanna. 'And you, my sister? Do you have dreams of love and a handsome husband?'

'Not yet, Zipporah. As you are the eldest, you must marry first, and then Gudit.' Tanna shrugged. 'When Gudit is married, then, perhaps, I can dream of a husband.'

The afternoon breeze lifted Zipporah's black hair. 'My husband will be strong, intelligent and kind.' She whirled about in a little dance. 'You are both right. I know that Father will choose my husband, but that doesn't stop me dreaming of how I hope the future will be.'

'Who will it be, Zipporah? Will you be happy with our father's choice?' her sisters teased her.

Life in Midian seemed very dull to the sisters. Every day they would spend the afternoons weaving and stitching the cloths which would be part of their dowries when they married.

Yet in her heart, Zipporah felt uneasy. She was only fourteen years old, and she did not feel ready to marry.

'Watch what you are doing,' warned her mother, Berhan. 'Some day you will be using this cloth in your own home.' She looked at Zipporah. 'Your father has started to look out for a suitable husband.'

Zipporah's eyes filled with tears. What could she say? What use were her dreams?

The afternoon sun was fading. 'It is time for you to take your father's flock to drink at the well.'

'I've nearly finished this cloth,' protested Zipporah. 'It only needs a few more stitches.'

Berhan smiled. 'The cloth and the stitches can wait,' she said. 'The animals will not.'

'The animals have to wait, Mother,' complained Zipporah. 'The shepherd boys push us aside and go first to the well. So we have to wait until they have finished, and so do the sheep.'

'The boys are rude,' joined in Gudit. 'They pretend they are going to touch us with their dirty, smelly hands, and when we run away, they laugh.' She scowled.

'Mother, you must speak to Father about it,' Zipporah pleaded. 'We are the daughters of the High Priest. The shepherd boys ought to treat us with respect.'

'Go on, go!' Berhan waved her hands. 'I will speak to your father, but for now, go! If you are made to wait and you come back late, then you can tell your father the reason for it.'

The girls hurried off. When they returned to the well with their sheep, they noticed a handsome stranger sitting in the shade of a palm tree. He appeared to be asleep. The girls felt uneasy; strangers very rarely came to this part of Midian. They usually spoke first to the High Priest, their father. Why hadn't this man done so? He wore the clothes of a wealthy Egyptian. What was he doing so far away from Egypt in the southern land of Midian?

They turned towards the well and began to fill the troughs for their father's flock. Suddenly several shepherd boys ran up, shouting, 'Out of our way, women!'

The girls moved quickly aside, driving their flock in front of them. 'Come, let's wait in the shade,' Zipporah called to her sisters. She hurried the sheep towards the oasis of trees and shrubs, and they watched while the shepherds gave water to their flocks.

The stranger now stood up. The shepherds hadn't noticed him before, and as he walked towards the well, his princely bearing frightened them, and they ran away.

The stranger beckoned the girls back to the well, where he filled their troughs for them. When the sheep had drunk enough, the girls hurried back home. They needed to tell their father about the stranger who had shown them such kindness. They whispered to each other as they ran. Never before had they seen a man like this.

Once the sheep were safely in their pen, the girls burst, out of breath, into the house, chattering and laughing. 'What's the meaning of this?' their father, Jethro, asked. 'How have you managed to return home so soon? Have you watered the sheep properly?' He looked at his eldest daughter.

'As we approached the well,' Zipporah explained, 'we saw a stranger from Egypt resting in the shade.'

'How did you know he was an Egyptian?'

'From his clothes, Father. They were beautifully made and woven from the finest cotton.' Zipporah and her sisters all smiled. 'The Egyptian chased the shepherds away and helped us fill the troughs.'

'And where is this Egyptian?' asked Jethro.

'We left him at the well.'

'Why did you leave this man alone when he had been so kind to you?'

'He is a stranger, Father.'

'True, but he helped you. Run back and fetch him,' Jethro told Zipporah. 'Invite him to break bread with your family.'

Zipporah flew like a bird to the place where she had left the Egyptian. 'It looks as if he is waiting for me,' she thought, and her heart started to beat faster. She led him back to her father's house, and stood aside as he exchanged greetings with Jethro. As she prepared a table and set food on it for their evening meal, she could not help turning to watch the two men talking to each other. Taking the wine from her mother's hands, she said, 'I'll do it.' And she smiled.

Slowly, the Egyptian told Jethro that his name was Moses. Although he had been born of Hebrew parents, he had been adopted by the Pharaoh's daughter and brought up as a prince in the Egyptian court. But one day he had seen an Egyptian soldier attacking one of the Hebrew slaves. Moses had rushed to help the slave, and in the heat of the moment he had killed the soldier, so now he feared for his life and had run away to the land of Midian.

Zipporah had never seen a man like him. If he was a prince, she wondered, why had he run away? How old was he? Her heart beat faster and her hands trembled as she served food to her father and his guest.

As darkness fell, Zipporah could see that Moses was relaxing in the safety of her father's house. Midian was so far south of Egypt that he knew the Pharaoh would not send his troops to look for a runaway prince here. After he had eaten he talked to Jethro, and it was decided that he would stay in Midian, and become the shepherd to Jethro's flock. It was not what he was used to as a prince, but he was relieved at Jethro's generous offer.

In the mornings, Moses helped the girls look after their father's sheep. He liked to stay close to Zipporah, and when their hands touched they would look into each other's eyes and smile. Zipporah sang with happiness and her heart danced. When the flock went to drink at the well, the shepherd boys kept at a respectful distance. Zipporah was pleased. She liked having Moses to protect her.

Jethro could see that Zipporah was falling in love with Moses, and he was anxious. This stranger admitted that he had killed an Egyptian soldier, and Jethro was worried that the Pharaoh would invade Midian if he heard where Moses was. Twice, he sent scouts to the border to see if soldiers were coming, but each time they returned saying that there were no signs and that all was well. Jethro stopped worrying and felt his heart warm towards Moses.

Springtime passed, and summer came. In the warm evenings, Zipporah and Moses walked together and talked to each other about everything that had happened in their lives. Zipporah asked Moses about his life at the Egyptian court; it sounded so exciting. As they walked, Moses took her hand to help her over the rocks on the path. Then he started to hold her hand all the time. As the summer days passed, their feelings for each other deepened and grew stronger. When autumn came in the second year in Midian, Moses asked Jethro for his daughter's hand in marriage. Berhan was not surprised. Like her husband, she had seen the way Moses and Zipporah looked at one another. She watched her six younger daughters dance round their sister, singing with happiness. The traditional gifts of wine and cake were brought out, and Jethro and Berhan blessed the young couple.

They began to get ready for the wedding. Because Moses was a stranger, he had no family to help with the preparations, but everyone in the village was related to Jethro, and they all joined in. In every home the women were busy cooking, for it was an honour to bring food to a royal wedding.

When the wedding day arrived, the elders gathered to act as witnesses. Jethro measured a white cord from the top of Moses's head to his toes. He then wound this round the groom's head as a sign of purity. He did the same to Zipporah, but this time it was a red cord, which was a sign of virginity. The ceremony had begun.

Zipporah felt like a princess in her beautiful soft wedding gown. Moses stood tall and handsome, looking like a prince, smiling at her. Jethro, as the High Priest, recited the marriage rituals, and Zipporah was filled with joy as she thought about the house which Moses had built for her. After his day's work with her father's flock, he had worked long into the night. He had insisted that the stones should be properly cut so that the building would stand securely. Often Zipporah had stayed with him, looking after the candles he used to light his work.

'Each night I work,' Moses had said, 'is one day closer to the time when you will be my wife.' His words delighted her, and she held the candles up high so that they would give more light.

Now the house was ready at last, and their wedding ceremony had started. Zipporah listened to her father's words. He raised his hands in blessing. Moses placed his ring on the first finger of Zipporah's right hand, and she was his wife.

The singing began, and the dancing. Everyone held hands and circled the young couple. Zipporah and Moses smiled at each other, and ate the cakes and drank the wine which promised a sweet life. The party lasted for seven days and six nights. Then, on the seventh night, by the bright light of the full moon, everyone walked behind the bride and groom as they made their way to their newly built house. They sang blessings to them — songs of happiness and peace. As Moses carried Zipporah into their home, Jethro whispered, 'Be fruitful and multiply.'

Winter came, and with it rain, but Zipporah knew her happiness was complete as she felt a baby growing inside her. Moses could feel their child kicking when he put his hand on to her tummy and he laughed out loud. When the time came for her to give birth, Zipporah went to the birthing hut where two midwives were waiting to help her. She cried out with joy when the women screamed the customary twelve shouts to tell everyone that a boy had been born.

When the baby was eight days old, she watched as Moses performed the duty of circumcision and sang, 'His name shall be Gershom, for it means "a stranger in this land".' Zipporah's thoughts flew back to the stranger who, not so long ago, had protected her and her sisters at the well.

When Gershom was two years old, Zipporah knew that the birth of her second child would be soon. 'My father said to be fruitful and multiply as you carried me into our new house after our wedding,' she reminded Moses.

'And so we are,' Moses answered. 'We have a child and another on the way, and even the flock of sheep has doubled in number.' He picked up Gershom. 'My son, your grandfather's flock needs to be taken close to the mountains where the grass is more plentiful.' He kissed his son, and said to Zipporah. 'I shall be gone for three days, no more, as I must be back to welcome our new baby.'

Hand in hand, the three walked to where the sheep waited to be driven to new pastures. Zipporah and Gershom waved as Moses disappeared into the distance, then they made their way to Jethro's house. Gershom ran happily in through the open door, sure of his welcome. Zipporah's sister Gudit was now married and was expecting her first baby, and preparations were being made for Tanna's wedding. The family home was full of love and excitement. But three days passed, then four, then five, and Moses did not return. As the time grew near for her to give birth, Zipporah became more and more anxious. Every day her fear increased. 'Send scouts to look for my husband,' she asked Jethro. But when they returned without news of him, everyone feared that he might be dead.

Zipporah cried as she gave birth to her second son, and she was still weeping seven days later when she left the birthing hut and returned to her father's house. The sun was shining but it did not make her feel any better. Jethro called his daughter to him. 'It is now a month since Moses left, and only the Lord knows what has happened to him,' he said softly. 'Your son is now three weeks old, and Moses was not here to circumcise him on the eighth day, as is the custom with our people.'

'Father,' wept Zipporah. 'I know Moses has met with misfortune.'

Jethro held her hand. 'We will continue to pray for his safe return.' He looked into his daughter's eyes. 'Since we don't know where Moses is, we shall have to postpone the baby's circumcision until he is in his thirteenth year. This is the law of the Midianites.'

Zipporah held her baby close, and wept again. Where was her husband? Was she a widow?

When she had recovered fully from the birth, she took her two sons and went back to her own house. The days crawled by. Zipporah kept thinking she could hear Moses's voice, and she would run outside to look for him.

Then, one morning when the sky was bright and clear, lo and behold, there was Moses leading Jethro's flock. Zipporah ran to him.

'Moses, Moses, you have come back. I thought you were dead,' she sobbed, tears of happiness running down her cheeks. 'How strange you look. What has happened?' She held up the new baby to show Moses, and Gershom peered out from behind her skirts.

Moses picked up his sons and held them tight. His eyes closed and he swayed back and forth whispering, 'My sons, my sons!' Then he opened his eyes and put Gershom down, and, still holding the baby, he reached for Zipporah. His body trembled with weariness.

'What happened, Moses?' Zipporah asked again. 'You have been gone for so long. Father sent out scouts to look for you, but they couldn't find you. It was as though you had vanished from the face of the earth.'

'I took Jethro's flock to the farthest end of the wilderness, to Mount Horeb,' Moses stammered. 'But I don't think you will believe what happened to me, Zipporah.'

'What happened to you?' she exclaimed. 'Tell me!' Moses looked so strange that she wasn't sure she really wanted to know.

'I came upon a bush that burned with a bright flame, a flame so strong that I felt it would burn my whole being. And, Zipporah, the bush was not consumed.' Moses took a deep breath. 'I heard a voice. A voice came from that burning bush.'

'The bush was speaking to you?'

'No, a voice spoke to me from the bush.'

'What did the voice say?' Zipporah found it difficult to believe what her husband was saying, and fear clutched at her heart.

'The voice told me to take off my shoes, for I stood on holy ground.'

Zipporah held Gershom and the baby close, and she trembled.

'The Lord spoke to me.'

'The Lord spoke to you?' Was her husband going mad? How could his God, who was invisible, speak to him?

'He spoke to me,' Moses said again. 'The Lord said that I must go back to Egypt and free my people.'

'Free your people?' Zipporah felt cold with fear. 'But Moses, if you return to Egypt you will be killed. My dear husband, think what you are saying!'

'I am saying, Zipporah, that in seven days' time we will set off for Egypt.'

Zipporah gasped. 'But I only had a baby four weeks ago.' She looked at her husband. He was exhausted. 'Let's talk about this later; just now you need rest.' And she led him into the house.

As Moses sat on the bed tiredness overcame him. 'My dearest ones,' was all he said. Then he leaned back, his head on the pillow, while Gershom slipped the sandals from his father's feet.

While Moses slept, Zipporah went to find Jethro. The things her husband had said frightened her. How was it possible for a man to speak with the Lord? What would happen if they went to Egypt? She was afraid that her husband would be killed and that she would be forced into slavery. And what would happen to her sons? Sobbing drowned out her words as she said all this to her father. She reached for his hand.

'Whatever happens, Zipporah, I shall take care of you. If danger faces you in Egypt, I shall rescue you.' Jethro's face was grave. 'But you must go with your husband.'

In the middle of the night Moses awakened. The room was filled with moonlight. Zipporah was asleep beside him, the baby in the curve of her arm. How beautiful they are, he thought. Would they be strong enough to come with him?

In the morning, Moses went to his father-in-law and told him what had happened in the wilderness. From his priestly chair, Jethro listened carefully. Was Moses mad or had the Lord really spoken to him?

'How can you be sure it was the Lord's voice you heard?' he asked.

'I was held in that place as though my feet were roots and my body a tree. The bush was on fire, but it was not consumed. I could see the flames, I could hear the flames.' Moses's eyes shone. 'And I heard the voice of the Lord. He knew everything that had happened to me in Egypt, and He told me what would happen when I went back.'

Jethro leaned forward. 'What did He say?'

'He told me to find my older brother, Aaron. He would help me.' Moses looked into Jethro's eyes. 'Let me go. I must return to Egypt and see if my kinfolk are still alive.'

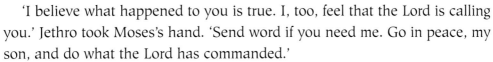

'I believe what happened to you is true. I, too, feel that the Lord is calling you.' Jethro took Moses's hand. 'Send word if you need me. Go in peace, my son, and do what the Lord has commanded.'

Zipporah was frantic with worry. She had never been away from her home, and both her husband and her father were insisting that she must go. She was anxious about travelling with two small children. She had hardly recovered from the baby's birth and she would have to ride on a donkey. She tried to find the right clothes and blankets and pillows to take with them to protect them from the desert winds and the stinging sand.

Gershom and Moses burst into the house, laughing. 'How can you laugh?' Zipporah scolded.

'I am laughing with happiness, for I am obeying the word of the Lord.'

'I do not want to go with you, Moses. I am afraid for myself and the children.'

'You are my wife, Zipporah. You must go with me. The Lord will protect us.'

The morning of their departure was at hand. Zipporah's donkey was piled with pillows to make it more comfortable for her. She held the baby, while Moses took Gershom on to his animal, which was loaded with food and water. They set off slowly — it would be a long journey to Egypt.

PASSOVER AND EXODUS

Each year, during the Holiday of Passover, a special celebratory meal called the Seder is served. In traditional Jewish households, a book called Haggadah is read to tell what to do and how to do it at the Seder meal. 'Haggadah' means 'telling a story'. To open the story, the children ask 'Why is this night different?'. The Passover Haggadah answers their question, for it is the story of how the Jews, who were once slaves, left Egypt and crossed the Red Sea to freedom.

~

At the Seder, symbolic foods are served to illustrate the story which makes this night different from all others. In their days as slaves, the Jews made bricks, held together with mortar, to build Pharaoh's monuments. Apples, nuts and raisins are ground together to represent this ancient mortar. It is sometimes formed into a pyramid and is eaten as the story of the Exodus is told. Bitter foods, such as horseradish root, are eaten, to recall the bitter life of the slave. Salt water, given to each member of the family in small dishes, represents the tears of oppression. Eggs, hard-boiled, shelled and set in salt water, are given to each person at the table. The eggs are symbolic of a new life and are eaten when the story of freedom is completed. Greens, usually parsley — a reminder of new growth — are also dipped in salt water and eaten. A roasted leg of lamb tells of the sacrifice of life and reminds everyone of the story of the bloodstained doorposts and how the Angel of Death passed over the homes of the Israelites. Matzah, dry biscuits made of flour and water, are also served, as a reminder of the Exodus and of the unleavened bread which was eaten by the fleeing Israelites.

~

Any stranger who comes to the door is welcomed in to partake of the Seder meal, for Jews remember that they were strangers in the land of Egypt. It is a time to remember slavery and oppression and to rejoice in freedom. This night is different because on this night, God delivered the Jews from slavery in Egypt.

MIRIAM
and
MOSES

It was a bright sunny day and Miriam was standing by the village well. She was now married to Caleb, and the mother of a fine, strong boy, Bezalel. In the distance she saw her brother Aaron walking towards her, accompanied by a stranger. Who was he? There was a little boy walking beside him, the same age as Moses had been when he went to live with Bithiah in the royal palace. There was a woman, too, riding a donkey and holding a baby.

As the group drew near, the stranger smiled. 'Miriam, it is I — Moses.'

'Moses! Moses! You have come back!'

Miriam welcomed Moses and his family into her home. After rest and food came the time for him to explain why he had returned.

'The Lord sent you!' wondered Miriam. 'What do you think Pharaoh will say? His heart is as hard as his brother's was. What will you say to him?'

'I will tell him that the Lord God of Israel has commanded me to tell him to free His children.'

Miriam was excited by Moses's words, and she ran from house to house telling the Israelites. But when her brothers returned from the palace, they had disturbing news. Not only had Pharaoh refused to free the Israelites but he had ordered the taskmasters to beat them even harder.

The next morning as the sun rose, Miriam could see Moses standing alone in the fields. He seemed to be talking to someone. Then he called to Aaron.

'Come, brother. The Lord has again told me to go to Pharaoh. I must say, "Let my people go or our Lord will inflict fearful punishments upon you."'

But again Pharaoh refused to listen to them.

'What will you do, Moses?' Miriam asked him.

'The Lord has told me to confront Pharaoh again when he goes to the river to bathe.'

Miriam followed her brothers as they went down to the river. She knew the path well, and she stayed back, but she could see Moses raising his rod high. She gasped, for the river had turned bright red and was giving off a foul smell. She ran home in fear.

When Moses and Aaron returned they announced, 'Pharaoh has released us; we are free.'

But their joy was short-lived. Pharaoh changed his mind.

Seven days later Miriam saw Moses and Aaron again preparing to confront Pharaoh. They would ask him to let the Israelites go free. Again, she followed at a safe distance, and watched them arguing with Pharaoh. This time it was Aaron who stretched out his rod over the waters. Miriam couldn't believe her eyes. There were frogs everywhere, even jumping on Pharaoh.

As she ran back home, Miriam was filled with dread at these strange happenings. Soon Moses and Aaron burst into the house. 'Zipporah, get our sons ready,' Moses called to his wife.

'Tell all the women, Miriam,' shouted Aaron. 'Pharaoh has relented. Our people are free!'

Miriam ran to the other houses in the village, calling out, 'We are free. Prepare to leave!'

When she returned home, she bundled up as many possessions as she, Caleb and Bezalel could carry. Zipporah gathered together the pillows and blankets to cushion her as she rode on the donkey. But once again Pharaoh broke his word and would not let the Children of Israel go.

Miriam was stunned. She wanted to leave so much that she stayed in her room for seven days, weeping bitter tears. She did not even cheer up when Moses told her that the Lord had sent swarms of flies to plague the Egyptians, nor when he told her that their bodies were now covered with terrible boils.

Each plague lasted for seven days but still Pharaoh would not let them go.

'Why do you go on believing Pharaoh when he promises to release us?' she asked Moses. 'What will happen to us?'

'The Lord knows of our suffering, sister,' Moses replied.

Miriam turned silently away from him.

Weeks later, Miriam and Zipporah and their friends were standing outside their home when Miriam saw darkness settling over the land.

'Miriam,' asked one of the women. 'Does Moses know about this strange darkness?'

'Yes,' she answered, 'just as he knew about the lice and the death of the cattle and the hail and the locusts.' She looked at the sky. 'It is the work of the Lord. It is another sign. I truly believe that He will save us.'

The darkness went on and on. Pharaoh called Moses and Aaron to the palace, and begged their forgiveness. He promised that this time he would allow the Israelites to leave.

Moses left the palace and pleaded with the Lord to lift the darkness, but as soon as the sun was shining again, Pharaoh went back on his word and once more denied the Israelites their freedom. And again Miriam shut herself in her room and wept.

The weeks passed and the cruelty of the Egyptians continued. One morning, Moses knocked on Miriam's door. When she let him in he again said softly, 'The Lord knows of our suffering.'

Miriam shook her head, her cheeks wet with tears. 'I have yet to hear His voice.'

'One day you will feel His presence.' Then Moses said with sadness, 'He has told me that He will go among the Egyptians and that every first-born will die.'

When day broke, Moses called all the Israelites together and spoke to them. 'This night, sacrifice a lamb, gather up a bunch of the herb hyssop, dip it into the blood of your sacrifice and splash it on your doorposts.' Moses paused. 'And none of you leave your houses until the morning.'

Miriam did not understand. 'Splash blood on the doorposts?'

'When the Lord comes among us to kill every Egyptian first-born — man, woman, child and beast — He will see the blood,' Moses said. 'He will pass over the houses of the Israelites.'

The people returned to their homes to do Moses's bidding. Caleb slaughtered a lamb and spread the blood on to the doorposts.

At midnight, Miriam was awakened by an eerie noise. It was a terrible howling sound, like a hundred voices moaning together as one. She shivered as she dressed and ran out of her room. Moses and Caleb stood together, their eyes wide and their faces flushed with excitement.

'What is that horrifying noise?' Miriam asked. 'Listen, it sounds like hundreds of human beings, crying and wailing.'

'It is the weeping of Pharaoh and his people,' said Moses. 'Every first-born, human and animal, is dying.'

Miriam remembered that Pharaoh himself had a son.

As they were eating breakfast the next morning, there was a loud shout. 'Pharaoh sends word,' a servant called. 'You must leave at once. Take your children and your flocks and be gone.' There was a silence. 'Leave!' he screamed. 'Death is among us!'

Miriam heard nervous shouts and the sound of running feet.

'We will leave when it is light,' said Moses.

When everything was ready, Miriam wrapped her kneading board and the unleavened bread-dough in a large white cloth. As the Israelites gathered in the early light, she looked with pride at her people. They were ready to walk to freedom. She took her place with her family at the front of the procession, close to Moses and his family.

She was startled by a sudden light. A pillar of fire appeared, as though leading the way. Moses spoke to it and all followed.

Miriam walked with a light step. She could hear the tinkling of her tambourine bells tucked up with her belongings. She smiled and spoke as though in prayer. 'Soon we will dance and sing of the wonders of our Lord.'

When they arrived at the sea, they all set down their belongings and prepared to rest. But then they heard a low rumbling sound, and they looked back towards Egypt. They could see a cloud of dust which hid the charging of Egyptian horses.

Miriam clasped Bezalel to her. 'Caleb, we are going to die! There is nowhere for us to go — the sea is in front of us and the Egyptians behind us!'

Caleb pointed. 'Look at your brother Moses.'

Miriam looked to her right. Moses was standing on the shore. He raised his rod and stretched it over the water. As she watched, the sea miraculously parted to make a pathway. A strong east wind blew, drying the sea floor.

'Come on, Caleb! Come on, Bezalel!' called Miriam. 'We will lead the people across with Moses.'

Zipporah carried baby Eliezer, while little Gershom followed her, leading the donkey. The water formed a wall to the right and a wall to the left. When they reached the other side, Miriam looked back. The Egyptians were pursuing them with horsemen, soldiers and chariots. They raced across the dry sea floor, towards the Israelites.

'Moses!' Miriam screamed. 'Save us!'

Moses stretched out his hand and the sea fell back into place. The great walls of water came crashing down on top of the Egyptian army, completely covering them. Not one soldier remained alive.

Miriam stood still. Now she believed what Moses had said. The Lord had protected the Israelites, and she believed that He would continue to protect them in days to come. She felt joy rising in her throat and she laughed aloud and reached for her tambourine. She raised it and shook it so that the tiny bells tinkled above her head. 'Sing! Sing!' she called.

All the women and children joined her, singing and dancing. The sound of their joyous voices filled the air as they circled round and round, singing their praise of the Lord and of their miraculous escape. Miriam's voice rose above the rest:

'Sing to the Lord! Sing to the Lord! The horse and rider He has thrown into the sea. The Lord has triumphed gloriously. Hallelujah!'

WOMEN AND THE LAW

*W*hen the Jews escaped from Egypt, they were a people who believed
in one God. The Commandments had not yet been given to them, nor had
the five books of Moses — the Torah — been written. The new laws
and ways of living developed as they wandered in the desert.

~

*The ethics of the Commandments had a powerful effect on the history of the
world, but no less important were the public health laws. The Jews knew how
to determine whether a person had leprosy (Lev. 12:2-17), they had a
practice for killing animals in a humane and clean manner (Lev. 17:2-7)
and a strict ethical code was established (Lev. 19:9-16).*

~

*In those days, all property was owned by men. If a man died, his possessions
were passed to his son. If he had no son, the property went to his brother.
Whoever inherited the property was legally obliged to take care of
the women and children of the family.*

~

*After the Ten Commandments had been delivered, the Jews wandered in the
desert for forty years. Towards the end of this period, as the Jews settled near
the Promised Land at the foot of Mount Nebo, five sisters questioned the laws.
Their father had died, leaving no sons, and they did not wish to be passed on
to their uncles or cousins as though they were just property. They argued their
case right through the judicial system, all the way to Moses himself, and they
won. It was ruled that a man's inheritance went first to his sons, but if there
were no sons, the daughters could inherit their father's property and goods.*

~

*Even after the daughters had won their rights of inheritance, however, there was
no change in the law regarding a wife who survived her husband's death.
The wife had no claim to property or to land. She had to live with
her sons or her late husband's brother.*

The DAUGHTERS of
ZELOPHEHAD

The five daughters of Zelophehad were in mourning. Two days before he died, their father had stumbled into their house, blood pouring from his head and running down his arms.

'Why has this happened?' wept Noah, the youngest.

'Only the Lord can answer that question,' answered Mahalah, touching her sister's hand.

'Enough weeping, little sister,' said Tirzah, the second daughter. 'We will honour our father best by looking after his land, his flocks and his home.'

'Will that bring our father back to us?' Noah looked at her through her tears.

'No,' Tirzah sighed. 'But it will give us a reason for living.'

The five daughters observed the usual time of mourning, and after thirty days, as they sat at the table, Noah asked what would happen to their father's land.

'The land was our father's,' said Milcha, 'so now it is ours.'

'We will have to be strong,' said Tirzah. 'Our uncle Manassah will claim it for his own, for only men can own land in our tribe.' She spread out her hands. 'But are not men and women equal in the eyes of our Lord?'

'We may be created equal in the Lord's eyes,' answered Hoglah, 'but in the eyes of the men of this tribe we are not!'

'If our uncle's family claims the land, what will happen to us?' asked Noah. 'Where shall we go? How shall we live?'

'We must go to Moses and claim our father's land,' insisted Milcha. 'But I am not sure whether Moses liked our father.'

'Had they quarrelled?' Noah's eyes widened with fear.

'If they had, I am afraid that Moses will give our inheritance to our uncle,' said Milcha.

'That must not happen!' Tirzah exclaimed loudly. 'We must stand before the entire congregation and present our case.'

'You must speak for us, Mahalah, as you are the eldest,' said Noah. 'You must present our case to the Chiefs of the Tribe.'

And so it was that, the next time the ten Chiefs of the congregation assembled at the door of the Tent of Meeting, they found the five daughters of Zelophehad waiting for them.

Mahalah spoke. 'Our father Zelophehad has died. He was a good man, and he taught us the ways of the Lord.' She paused. 'We have come to ask you for justice, and the right to inherit his land.'

The ten Chiefs were taken aback by the fearless way this young woman spoke to them.

'This is a case of inheritance,' said one.

'It is not within our scope,' said another.

'This must be settled by a higher authority,' said a third.

Disappointed, the sisters turned for home, but they were determined not to give up their claim. The next day they came again to the Tent of Meeting. This time, fifty Chiefs were assembled.

'Our father believed in the Lord,' began Mahalah. 'He believed in the Law which Moses brought us from the Lord. And we believe that we are our father's rightful heirs.'

Once again, the Chiefs said, 'We cannot judge this matter. You must go to a higher authority.'

Days passed. The sisters were worried, yet confident that their voices would be heard. When they again approached the Tent of Meeting, they found that thousands of Chiefs had assembled. But even they could not give the daughters of Zelophehad the answer they wanted. Finally, Mahalah, Tirzah, Hoglah, Milcha and Noah went to Eleazar, the High Priest.

'Our father has died,' said Mahalah. 'He always obeyed the Lord's law. We only want what is our rightful inheritance.'

The High Priest listened carefully to her, but he, too, felt he could not decide the matter. Suddenly he saw Moses walking towards him. 'Look, there is Moses, our Teacher! He will know the answer.'

The five daughters stood before Moses, before Eleazar, the High Priest, before the princes and before the entire congregation at the door of the Tent of Meeting.

Mahalah spoke for her sisters. 'Our father has died. He always obeyed the Law.' She looked directly at Moses. 'He had no sons. It seems wrong that his daughters cannot continue to own his land and his flocks. We ask to be able to inherit them for ourselves.'

Moses knew that all the learned men of Israel, all the heads of families, all the princes, had shown respect for the Law, so he said, 'I cannot judge this matter as I, too, have a superior.'

Then Moses entered into the Tent of Meeting and prayed to the Lord. The Lord listened and spoke to Moses. 'The daughters of Zelophehad are right. You shall give them their father's land and possessions. But when they marry, they must choose husbands from within their own tribe. This is the law: if a man dies without sons, you shall transfer his property to his daughters. If he has no daughters, then his brother shall inherit. If he has no brothers, then the property shall go to his nearest relative.'

Moses came out of the Tent of Meeting and announced to the assembled people: 'The Lord has commanded that the daughters of Zelophehad shall inherit their father's property. But, so that the property stays within their tribe, they must marry men of their tribe.'

Mahalah, Tirzah, Hoglah, Milcha and Noah nodded in agreement. And when they married they chose men from among their relatives, so that the land stayed within their family.

Because of their courage and persistence, the women of Israel have been able to inherit the lands of their fathers to this day.

A JEW BY CHOICE

*O*ne of the great strengths of the Bible is that many of the stories apply
to the problems of the modern world. Today, Jewish people often have to
deal with the challenge of marrying a person of a different faith.
The Book of Ruth tells the result of a marriage of this kind
which occurred before the time of King David.

~

Ruth was born in the land of Moab in about 1200 BC. She married a Jew
who had come to her land with his parents. They were Israelites seeking to
escape from a famine in Bethlehem and to find food and work in Moab.
Her mother-in-law was called Naomi, and when her husband and sons
died, Naomi wanted to return home to Bethlehem. Ruth refused to let her
mother-in-law travel alone and she accompanied her back to Israel.

~

Under Jewish law, neither Ruth nor Naomi was entitled to an inheritance.
They became the responsibility of the next male in line, known as the
redeemer, who was obliged to look after them.

~

When she left Moab to travel with Naomi to Israel, Ruth became a Jew by
choice. In Bethlehem, she married her husband's kinsman, a Jew called Boaz.
Their son was Obed, who was the father of Jesse, who in turn became the father
of David, who was to become King David. So it was that Ruth, who had
converted to Judaism, became the maternal ancestor of the House of David.
She is still warmly remembered for her love and devotion to Naomi,
and for her readiness to abandon a life of privilege and set out with
Naomi for a strange new land.

R U T H

Summoned by their father, King Eglan of Moab, Orpah and Ruth hurried through the palace halls, their silken robes billowing behind them. Servants ran before them, calling, 'Hurry! Hurry! The king awaits you!'

Ruth's heart beat wildly. An urgent call from the king. What had happened?

Outside the throne room, the two girls paused to catch their breath. They looked at each other. 'Why has our father ordered us to come to the throne room?' questioned Orpah, the eldest. 'This is where our country's events are planned and where the king meets his important visitors.'

'I have no idea,' answered Ruth, uneasily. 'Do you think that our mother, the queen, has been summoned as well?'

Before Orpah could answer, the Royal Guard bowed low and opened the tall golden doors. The princesses respectfully approached and bowed before their father.

'My daughters,' smiled King Eglan. 'You have been honoured and you have been chosen. You have been chosen not by royal decree, but by our citizens.'

'What is he talking about?' Ruth thought. She was afraid of what her father meant by 'chosen'.

The two girls bowed again, their heads touching the tile floor.

'The family of Elimelech, a wealthy Israelite, settled in our fair land several years ago when a famine struck Israel.' He paused and looked at his daughters.

Ruth was puzzled. What had this family to do with her? She was of royal blood! She lifted her chin a little higher.

'The father has died, leaving his widow and two sons,' the king went on. 'The sons, Machlon and Kilion, have inherited their father's wealth, and own a great deal of land. I know them well. They are both most intelligent.'

Ruth and Orpah looked at each other and shrugged. What did this have to do with them?

'The two young men were taken by your beauty,' King Eglan smiled. 'They have asked for your hands in marriage.'

'Marriage?' Ruth cried out, beginning to shake. 'No, Father, that cannot be right! My life, what will happen to my life?' She could not control her fear. 'Does our mother know about this?'

'No, the queen is not involved in affairs of state.'

'Aiii!' Orpah threw herself on to the floor. 'I am not an affair of state,' she screamed. 'I am your daughter! We are princesses!' She lay kicking and shrieking as though her shouts would change everything.

'Father,' gasped Ruth, 'what was your answer?'

'They are willing to pay a great deal of money and much of their lands for two Moabite princesses.'

'Yes,' groaned Ruth, 'but, Father, what was your answer?'

'Of course I agreed. Our treasury is weak. Their money will strengthen it. You will both sacrifice your crowns for the sake of your country.'

'We will sacrifice not only our crowns but our bodies,' cried Ruth.

'Oh,' moaned Orpah from the floor, her arms now covering her head. 'Father, we are too young to marry. It is only a year since I became a woman, and Ruth is even younger.'

The king frowned. 'You are not too young. Your mother was your age when I married her. And,' he announced, 'I will perform the wedding myself.'

And so it was that the two Moabite princesses reluctantly and fearfully married the two men from Judah, while the grooms' mother, Naomi, watched. They need not have been afraid, however, for their husbands were loving and attentive. Their own mother was often ignored by their father as he had other wives, and they thought their husbands would behave in the same way, but

they were wrong. Orpah and Ruth lived with their husbands in large houses, with servants to do their bidding, fine gowns and rich food. They lacked for nothing. Then, suddenly, after ten years of marriage, both husbands were struck down by strange fevers and they died.

For a whole year, Orpah and Ruth grieved for their lost husbands, and Naomi wept at losing both her sons. Ruth could sense her mother-in-law's anguish, as together they performed the religious rites of the Israelites for their dead.

'You need not suffer with me, Ruth. I am their mother,' Naomi often said.

'Your son was my husband and you are still my mother-in-law,' Ruth said. 'We may not be connected by blood, but we are connected by love.' She paused. 'While I do not fully understand the Hebrew prayers which you chant, allow me to stand with you so that we do not feel our pain alone.'

The day came when Naomi felt that her time in Moab was over. She must go home to Judah. When she told her daughters-in-law, Ruth quickly responded, 'My father, the king, will look after us as he has in this year of grief. We will be able to go on living as we have in the past. There is no need to return to Judah, Naomi.'

'No, Ruth.' Naomi shook her head. 'I feel I must go back. The famine has long passed and the country is prosperous once more. I must return to the land once owned by my husband.'

'Orpah and I cannot leave you, Naomi. You have loved us and shown us kindness.' Ruth reached for her mother-in-law's hand. 'You have taught us to care for the sick and the poor. We have learned to teach the lame to work with their hands. You have given us so much.' She shook her head. 'We cannot allow you to return to Judah alone.'

'But, Ruth, you and Orpah were raised in a royal household. You are princesses.'

'Remember, Naomi? We gave up our crowns when we married your sons.'

'The three of us have lived well here, wanting nothing,' Naomi said. 'Life in Judah is hard. I do not know if the land I left will still belong to me.'

'Naomi, it is too dangerous for you to go alone,' said Orpah. 'Ruth and I fear for you. We must come with you.'

The king was furious. 'Leave Moab?' he shouted. 'Leave your land, your heritage?' he ranted. 'Then you will leave all your royal belongings, all your jewels. You will leave Moab penniless.'

But Orpah and Ruth were determined to go with Naomi, and for four weeks they prepared for the journey, then they set out on the road together. They were not dressed like wealthy women. Their clothing was simple so as to withstand the heat and light and not to be a burden on their slender shoulders. It was late afternoon when they came to an oasis. Tired, they stopped to eat and rest. Ruth went to the well for water. She filled the water bags and took wet cloths back to Naomi and Orpah so that they might wipe the dust from their faces and the sand from between their toes.

Again, Naomi questioned her daughters-in-law. 'I feel you would both be happier returning to your father's palace. Do not stay with me out of duty.' Three times she urged them to turn back, and each time they refused, but the next time Orpah weakened. 'Oh Ruth,' she whispered, 'I am not as strong as you are.' The sisters held each other and sobbed. They knew this would be their final separation. Orpah kissed Ruth and Naomi goodbye and turned back towards her father's palace.

Naomi took Ruth in her arms. Then she spoke. 'Ruth! In Judah you cannot live as my Moabite daughter-in-law and you cannot live as a Moabite princess. If you come with me you will have to accept Judaism as your way of life. Are you sure that is what you want?'

'Wherever you go, I will go,' answered Ruth.

When Naomi shook her head, Ruth continued, 'Wherever you live, I will live.'

'It will be difficult,' whispered Naomi.

'Your people will be my people,' Ruth smiled at her mother-in-law. 'And Naomi, when it is your time to die, I will be with you. And when it is my time to die, I will be buried with you.'

When Naomi saw how determined Ruth was, she stopped arguing. They continued on their journey, but it was dangerous for women to travel alone without a man to protect them, so they disguised themselves in men's clothing.

The road was rough and the rocks cut their sandalled feet and the desert sand stung their skin. At last they reached Bethlehem, and people welcomed Naomi, but when she presented Ruth as Machlon's widow she was looked upon as a stranger, and given no words of welcome. Dirty and exhausted, the

women were a pitiful sight. Ruth saw the faces of Naomi's former neighbours, and she heard their whispers. 'Can this be Naomi?' asked one woman.

'Barefoot and in rags?' said another. 'And with a Moabite daughter-in-law!'

Ruth put a comforting arm around Naomi. 'When I left here,' Naomi said to the women, 'I was happy with a wealthy husband and two fine sons. I have returned a widow with no sons, but with a loving daughter-in-law.'

'And together we will build a new life,' said Ruth.

They walked through the streets to Naomi's former home. It had been well built and its stone walls were just as she had left it more than ten years before. The two women were soon sleeping soundly on dusty, bare beds.

In his absence, Elimelech's land lay unworked and barren. Now he and his sons were dead and Ruth wondered who owned the land. Naomi and Ruth had only a very little money, enough to feed them for one day.

Ruth took Naomi's hand. 'I am not too proud to work. Although I have never had to before, I will soon learn.'

'Please be careful.'

'I will be careful, Naomi. I will go out to the fields and glean as much barley as I can find.'

'Find fields where you are sure that the owner will allow you,' cautioned Naomi.

Early the next morning Ruth walked out to the fields carrying a large basket, which Naomi had found. She stopped at the first field she came to. There was no owner for her to ask permission from, but, because she was a widow, she was allowed to glean the fallen grain and no one approached her. Quickly, she began to gather the stalks of barley which the harvesters had forgotten. She stayed well behind the other workers so that no one would take any notice of her. When she felt too tired to continue, she sat on the ground and beat the barley seeds from the stalks she had gathered. These she put in the basket, leaving the heavy stalks on the ground. Every day she returned to the same field.

By chance, Ruth had chosen to glean in a field belonging to Boaz, who was a kinsman of Elimelech's. One morning Boaz returned from his business in the city and greeted his workers, 'Peace be with you.'

Smiling they answered, 'Peace be with you, Boaz.'

Then he noticed Ruth. She was the only woman gleaning at the time and he assumed she was related to one of the harvesters. Her beauty and her graceful manner aroused his curiosity, so he asked his overseer who she was.

'She is a Moabite girl,' he answered. 'She is the one who returned with Naomi.'

Boaz nodded. 'They are both widows. Let her stay.'

47

The next morning, when Ruth returned to the field, Boaz approached her. She bowed in respect.

'I am pleased you are here,' he said. 'You may go to the field where the girls are working, and if you are thirsty help yourself to water from the jug.'

Ruth lowered her head. 'Thank you for your kindness, sir.'

'It is to thank you for your kindness to my relative, Naomi, your mother-in-law. You have treated her with compassion and gathered grain for her and protected her.'

When the workers stopped for their midday meal, Boaz asked her to eat with him at the head of the table, but Ruth did not want the other workers to think she was any different from them, so she stayed with the reapers with whom she worked. She took very little food, but Boaz noticed her empty plate and handed food to her. Politely, she ate, but when she had had enough, she set some aside to take home to Naomi.

When they had finished eating and the workers returned to the field, Boaz told the men in charge, 'Drop stalks of barley as though by accident. Allow her to take as much as she needs.' Ruth was very careful, however, not to take too much grain.

When Naomi saw the amount of barley Ruth had collected and the food

from the afternoon meal, she knew that Ruth must have been gleaning in the fields of a friendly owner. 'Where did you work today?' she asked.

'In fields which belong to a man called Boaz. He is a most generous man and gave me extra food.'

Naomi laughed. 'Boaz is the nephew of my late husband. He has always been a fine man.'

Ruth nodded. 'He is certainly kind to me.'

'Boaz is closely related to us. In fact, under our laws, he is in line to take possession of this house. As a widow, I have no claim to it or to my husband's land. My husband's brother, Tov, has the first claim as next-of-kin.'

'That does not seem right. Is there any way you can regain ownership of this house?'

'As a woman, I have no rights, but perhaps Boaz will help us.'

The barley season lasted for three months and Naomi was afraid that Boaz would forget about Ruth. He was a wealthy landowner, a judge and a leader of his community. Naomi was poor and Ruth was a foreigner, only recently converted to Judaism. Naomi felt that he needed to be reminded of his responsibility to the family of his dead uncle, Elimelech.

When harvesting was over and the winnowing completed, there came word that a band of robbers might try to steal the grain, so on the final night of the harvest Boaz decided to sleep on the threshing-room floor and guard his grain. Naomi suspected that he might, and she had a plan which she hoped would ensure Ruth's and her own future life. After they had finished their evening meal, she spoke to Ruth. 'Although I am only your mother-in-law, I feel as though you are my own daughter.'

'And my feelings towards you are those of a daughter.'

'Ruth, I want a good life for you and a good marriage. You are too young to remain a widow, and Boaz is a widower.'

'What do you mean, Naomi?'

Naomi looked into Ruth's eyes. 'Because there have been thefts in this neighbourhood, tonight Boaz will sleep on the threshing-room floor. I have a plan. You should bathe, dress in your Sabbath clothes and go to the threshing-room. Remain hidden until you are certain Boaz is asleep.' She leaned closer

and whispered the rest of her plan. 'You must uncover his feet and then lie down at them.'

'But why, Naomi? I do not understand.'

'In Jewish law, a brother or an uncle has a moral obligation to marry his brother's or his nephew's widow. In our case,' said Naomi, 'the redeemer is my brother-in-law, Tov. However, Ruth, by lying at his feet, you will be reminding Boaz of his duty.'

Ruth felt very uneasy about Naomi's plan, but because she loved her she agreed to do it. So, in the middle of the night, she walked to the threshing-room. She was frightened. She tiptoed in and found the sleeping Boaz. She uncovered his feet as Naomi had told her to do and lay down. The wooden floor was still warm after the heat of the day.

Time passed. Ruth felt that her actions were shameful. She wondered what Orpah would say. She remembered her comfortable life in her father's palace. She could hear Boaz's steady breathing. Suddenly, he turned over and his foot brushed against her head. Startled, he sat up. 'Who is there?' he called out in a loud voice, reaching for his stick.

'I am your servant, Ruth, sent here this night by Naomi. Spread your robe

50

over me, Boaz.' And so they spent the night together, but Boaz did not touch her for he knew that she was a virtuous woman. By daylight, she was gone, taking with her Boaz's promise of marriage.

As the day brightened, Boaz went to the city gates where the elders gathered to discuss local affairs and to settle arguments between citizens. When Tov, Naomi's brother-in-law, appeared, Boaz called to him, 'Come and sit with me.'

Tov seated himself next to him against the stone wall.

Boaz said, 'You are next in line to inherit the parcel of land which belonged to Elimelech.'

'Yes, I know,' said Tov.

'Naomi has brought with her a daughter-in-law, a Moabite named Ruth. If you take back the land, you will also take on responsibility for Naomi and for Ruth.'

'I cannot do that. I have a wife and children. Take the land and the women for yourself, Boaz.'

'Done!' said Boaz.

Tov took off his sandal and handed it symbolically to Boaz. 'As I hand over my shoe, so I hand over my claim to the land.'

Boaz turned to the town elders. 'All of you are witnesses,' he said as he waved the sandal in the air. 'And I have also gained Ruth for my wife.'

And so it was that Ruth and Boaz were married, and nine months later a son was born, whom they named Obed. He in his turn became the father of Jesse, who was the father of David. That same David, great-grandson of Ruth and Boaz, became King David of Israel.

WOMEN AND MARRIAGE

The first Jewish king was Saul. Among his favourite subjects was a young man called David, who was renowned for his diligence as a shepherd, his talents as a musician and poet and most of all for his famous battle with the Philistine champion, Goliath, whom David slew with a stone flung from a sling. A misunderstanding caused Saul to force David into exile. David later became King of Judea and then King of all Israel, but at that time he was forced to lead a desperate life in which he and his men had to eke out an existence. They were probably considered to be bandits by the local inhabitants whom they approached for gifts of food.

~

One incident between David and a wealthy sheep-owner, Nabal, introduces us to Abigail, considered to be one of the most beautiful women in the Bible.

~

David's reign began in about 1000 BC. What rights did women have at that time? The story of Abigail shows us that a married woman could not leave her husband, no matter how harshly he treated her. However, she did take charge of all domestic affairs. Abigail was able to use her power as mistress of the household to go against her husband's wishes and act in a way that she felt was fair. Unfortunately, in this day and age, there are still many who demand that women follow these customs. However, many women in today's world now live in less patriarchal societies and know what it means for a woman to be free to live and act on her own terms. Abigail is a role model both for these women and for their less liberated sisters. She defied the accepted traditions of her time and took a huge personal risk when she acted against her husband's will by helping David.

A B I G A I L

'Mother, who is that strange looking man talking to my father?' whispered Abigail. 'Do you know him?' She stared. She had never seen a man like him.

'All I know is that he is from Carmel and his name is Nabal.'

'Nabal? But that means "crudeness". What a strange name to give a child.'

'Whatever the name,' said her mother as she glanced over to where the men sat, 'he appears to be quite wealthy.' She nodded towards the window and looked out. 'He has brought several sheep as a gift for your father.'

The two finished kneading the dough that would be bread for their evening meal, and Abigail pressed it into a clay pot. Her mother placed the pot on top of a cauldron filled with burning coals. Abigail felt uneasy, almost afraid of her mother's answer. 'Do you know why he is here, Mother?'

'I believe he is asking your father for your hand in marriage.'

'Abigail!' her father called.

She swallowed the lump in her throat. 'O Lord, I beg of you, watch over me,' she whispered.

Holding her breath, Abigail walked into the room. The man was twice her size, with wild black hair and a thick beard.

'Abigail, this is Nabal,' her father said. 'He has heard of your beauty, your goodness and your piety.'

Nabal smiled. His teeth shone white behind his black beard. To Abigail, he looked like a wild animal that wanted to eat her, and a shiver ran down her spine. She clenched her fists to keep herself from trembling. She felt so small. This man seemed like a giant. She swallowed her tears and looked down at the floor.

Her father beamed. 'You will be marrying into great wealth, Abigail.'

She wanted to cry out, 'Happiness is the greatest wealth. How can this man make me happy?' But she remained silent.

'Ah yes,' Nabal said in his deep voice. 'I have a large house, two hundred servants, three thousand sheep, one thousand goats, and all the wool from the shearing.'

At the next full moon, Abigail became Nabal's wife. The following day, at sunrise, they left for his home in Carmel. Abigail turned away from her husband. She was frightened. She had never been away from home before. She did not know this man with whom she would be spending the rest of her life. What was the use of wealth if it meant losing her freedom? She shivered, and prayed silently, 'May the Lord bless me and protect me.'

As the sun set and they rode into the courtyard of Nabal's home, Abigail felt a little less uneasy. Cheerful servants and congratulatory neighbours welcomed them with flowers and song. There was a lavish meal set ready, and everyone feasted, and drank wine from Nabal's vineyards.

'Drink up, Abigail.' Nabal's speech was already slurred. 'Drink up. Drink the wine,' he repeated.

Abigail pulled away from him. 'You have drunk enough for two of us already.' She was frightened of his drunkenness.

'Do you hear my child-bride?' Nabal laughed, and his voice thundered out. 'She says I have had too much to drink!'

One of his friends laughed, too. 'You have taken a wife to love, but wait until she learns how much more you love wine.'

Abigail glared at him. She hated being there. She hated that man, and she hated Nabal. She turned to her husband, who was drinking wine as though it were water. She was afraid.

'Husband, may I leave?' she said, softly. 'It has been a long day, and I am tired.'

'Did you hear that?' Nabal shouted to his guests. 'My young bride wishes to leave our wedding feast!'

The men laughed. The women of the house looked at Abigail to see what she would do. Abigail stared down at her hands, folded in her lap, and felt very alone. There was no one to help her; she must help herself. She stood up and said firmly, 'Forgive me if I leave, my husband.'

Nabal towered over her. 'You are shaming me.' His words were slurred. 'Our guests are still eating — your husband is not ready to leave the table.'

He took her wrist and pulled her down beside him. 'Sit down, wife. You may leave when I am ready to leave.'

Abigail was afraid of her husband. She dreaded his return from the fields each evening, but she did as she was bidden. She did not want to anger him, for then he would hit her.

When spring came and the fields showed green again, it was time to begin shearing the sheep. Nabal worked with his shearers, as his flock was large.

At noon, Abigail and her women loaded up the donkeys with food and drink for the workers, and took them out to where they were shearing. As they were returning home, they were followed by a young man.

'Are you Nabal's wife?' he asked Abigail.

'Yes, I am.' Abigail looked at the young man. 'You are a stranger to me. What do you want?'

'I am with David, the son of Jesse,' he said.

Abigail nodded. She had heard of David.

'We are camped in the wilderness and we need food,' the young man continued. 'David sent ten of us to approach Nabal, greet him by name and tell him we come in peace, but he refused us food and sent us away angrily. He said he needed the bread, meat and wine for his men. He refused to share it with us.'

'Have you told David what he said?'

'Yes. My master was angry. He ordered every man to prepare for battle.'

'My husband does not know the ways of the Lord.' Abigail shook her head. 'Wait here.' She hurried into the house, and called to her servants to prepare a great quantity of food. She knew she was disobeying her husband, but it was wrong to refuse food when there was plenty. She worked with the women. 'Food in exchange for war,' she told them.

When everything was ready, they loaded the animals with two hundred loaves of bread, two skins of wine, five dressed sheep, five bushels of grain, one hundred clusters of raisins and two hundred cakes of figs. Abigail told the young man to lead the way. She would follow seated on her donkey. 'Be careful,' she said. 'We must go secretly, for Nabal will be very angry. We must not let him see what we are doing, or surely there will be blood shed.'

They rode up into the mountains. The young man looked back several times. Abigail waved to him to show she was safe. The young man led the donkeys down into a thicket where he met David and his men. Abigail held tightly on to her donkey and slowly descended the steep path into the valley. When he saw her, David strode towards her and helped her down. She bowed in respect and said, 'I pray thee, my lord, accept this food from the house of Nabal.'

'Nabal?' David seemed puzzled. 'But he refused us food. He did not know me, nor Saul who came before me.'

'Forgive my husband, my lord, he doesn't know the ways of the Lord.' She looked up into David's face. 'Please accept these gifts from your servant, Abigail.'

'You are Nabal's wife?'

Abigail felt ashamed of her husband. 'My husband behaves rudely, like his name. He is cruel and crude, but, my lord, you are a powerful man and one day you will rule over Israel. Do not raise your hand against Nabal — you would not be fighting the battle of the Lord. Yours would be revenge for the way Nabal has treated you. There is no need for bloodshed.' She bent her head and blushed for speaking out so boldly.

David looked at her for a long time. His face was serious when he spoke again. 'I have been blessed, Abigail, that the Lord sent you to meet me this day. You have stopped me from doing wrong. If you hadn't come, I would have destroyed Nabal and all his people, including you.'

Abigail closed her eyes and looked down. David put out his hand and turned her face towards his. Through her tears, Abigail heard him say, 'Go in peace. You have shown me the way of gentleness. We will surely meet again.' He lifted her up, placed her on the donkey's back, and, putting the reins into her hand, he said again, 'Go in peace.'

When she arrived home, she found that Nabal and his men had finished shearing and had gathered to celebrate. Abigail was worried. Had Nabal discovered what she had done? But the mood was festive, there was plenty of food and drink, and the men seemed happy. Nabal's loud voice rose above the rest.

'Ah, you are just in time,' he said to Abigail. He raised his bowl of wine to his mouth and then offered it to her.

'I do not want any wine,' she said.

'And why is that?' Nabal grabbed her wrist. 'Is my wine not good enough for you?' He pulled her towards him. 'Did you know that David had sent his men begging for my food and my wine?'

Abigail was too afraid to answer him directly. Instead she said, 'You should eat something, Nabal. You have had too much to drink.'

'You can never have too much!' and Nabal refilled his bowl.

Abigail hurried to her room. As she lay on her bed and wept, she wondered how her father could ever have given her in marriage to such a drunken fool.

The next morning, as Nabal ate breakfast, she told him about her meeting with David.

'How did you meet David?' he shouted, his face contorted with anger.

'One of his men came here. He told me that David was preparing to attack you.'

'Attack me?' Nabal stood up, food clinging to his beard. He pounded the table with his fists. 'His men came begging for food. They wanted the food I had provided for my shearers.' His voice rose in anger, and he paced the room. 'Why should I feed David's men?'

'I took them food, Nabal.' Abigail's voice was soft, fearful of her husband's wrath.

'You!' he shrieked. 'You took David food after I, your husband, had refused him?' Spittle encircled his mouth. He shook his clenched fists at her.

'I saved us from a battle, Nabal.' Abigail's voice was now strong. She felt she must speak. 'If I had not taken food to David, he would have killed you and all your men.'

'Killed me?' he screamed. 'You went against my word!' Abigail felt Nabal's fist slam against her head and she fell to the ground. Eyes closed, she remained still. If she moved, she was afraid he would kill her.

'You are my wife!' he shouted. 'You will do as I say. Do you hear me? You will do as I say!' Suddenly, Nabal choked, gasped, and fell to the floor, groaning.

Abigail raised her head. Nabal lay clutching his chest, his anguished eyes wide open.

'Nabal,' she whispered, not knowing what to do, still afraid of his blows. She waited, but the only sound was Nabal's gasping groans. Slowly, she stood up. He still had not moved. Abigail called the servants to carry him to his bed, where he lay as one turned to stone.

Ten days later, Nabal was dead.

Abigail remained in the house, observing and completing the necessary days of mourning. She shed no tears of regret. She felt that she had fulfilled her marriage vows as best she could.

Some time afterwards, on a bright day, Abigail saw two young men approaching her house. She went out to meet them. They bowed before her.

'We bring word from our lord, David. He sends you greetings. He remembers you kindly.' They moved nervously. 'David has sent us to ask if you will return with us.'

'Why would I do that?' she replied.

One young man looked up to the skies as though searching for an answer. Then he faced Abigail. 'Now that you are free, David has asked if you will be his wife.'

Abigail's heart leaped within her body. She remembered how she had felt when she met David. She smiled, but she said, 'I must think about this honour. Please come back in seven days and I will give David his answer.'

For seven days she walked in the fields surrounding Nabal's house. She thought about the miserable life she had led and the kind of life that marriage with David promised. When the young men returned, she stood tall and said, 'I am ready to serve David as his wife and I will go with you to join him.'

She called five of her servants, who prepared the animals, taking everything they would need for her future life. They followed David's messengers, singing songs of blessings to the Lord. They sang clearly, for the Lord had watched over Abigail. They sang sweetly, for the Lord had brought them to safety with promises of peace.

Abigail and David were married. When he became king, they lived in Hebron. Abigail became queen and gave birth to a son, Daniel.

THE LIVING WORD

O f all the righteous women in the Bible, only one, Huldah, was considered to be a prophet. Huldah lived during the reign of King Josiah in about 620 BC, and was related to the prophet Jeremiah. It is said that Jeremiah taught the Torah to the men and that Huldah taught the Torah to the women.

~

According to the Bible, Solomon's Temple had fallen into disrepair and was being restored by order of King Josiah. Workmen found a scroll buried in the foundations which foretold the destruction of the Temple because God's law was not being obeyed — many of the Jewish people had forgotten God and had begun to worship idols. In 586 BC, the Babylonians destroyed Solomon's Temple. The Jews were exiled but, thanks to the teachings of Jeremiah and Huldah, they were able to take the living word of the Torah with them, and so the true faith survived. Even now, Jewish people carry their literature with them, including the Torah and the other books of the Bible, the Talmud, Midrash and the Apocrypha. The Dead Sea Scrolls are the oldest written record of many of these texts.

~

Jewish people study the Torah throughout their lives. Today, many Jews join religious study groups at their synagogue. The education of children, however, begins at home. On Friday evenings, there is a Sabbath service, where candles are lit and blessed and blessings are said over the wine. Then the whole family sings a blessing of the bread. There are also religious holidays — the Purim celebration, the Passover Seder and the building of the Succot — when children learn about Jewish history, law, ethics and morals. Formal Jewish education for children is given by scholars and rabbis. At the age of thirteen, a Jewish child is considered to be an adult and a ceremony called Bar Mitzvah (for boys) or Bat Mitzvah (for girls) marks the occasion when the young person reads from the Torah for the first time. Bat Mitzvah is a modern custom; more traditional Jewish communities have a ceremony for girls called Bat Chayil in which the girl accepts her responsibilities as a Jewish woman.

HULDAH

From the doorway of her house in the hills above Jerusalem, Huldah could see the crowd. Even from that distance, she could make out what they were saying, and the voices sounded bitter.

'It is true? A boy of eight is to be king?'

'Still at his mother's breast!'

'Who is he?'

'He is King Manasseh's grandson — the son of King Amon. You know what that means!'

Huldah shook her head. She thought about the reigns of Manasseh and Amon. They had spread terror among their subjects, destroying their temples and killing thousands of innocent people. They had not followed the teachings of the Lord. Would a small child be able to rescue his lost people? She went back into her house, the peace and quiet comforting her. 'King Josiah, I wish you well,' she said.

The land of Judah had suffered greatly during the recent past. Josiah's father and grandfather had not followed the faith of their fathers. They had tried to stamp it out. They had removed from the Temple the Sacred Ark containing the Laws which had been given to Moses by the Lord. They had desecrated the Holy of Holies, and sacrificial tables displaying obscene idols had been left standing. Huldah shivered as she thought of the fate of the

prophet Isaiah who had tried to warn the people. He had met a martyr's death by the tyrant's furious sword.

She felt her age as she walked carefully out into her garden, but she smiled when she saw her loom, suspended between two trees. It looked like an old friend. She added two blue threads to her new weaving. 'One for you, Josiah, and one for your mother, Jedidah.' Huldah pulled the strands tightly through the warp. 'May Jedidah teach you the ways of your ancient religion. And here are two more blue threads with prayers that you, Josiah, may enable the people to return to the glorious days of King Hezekiah.'

Josiah's great-grandfather, Hezekiah, had smashed the idols, cleansed the Temple of Solomon, and taught the True Religion to the people. Would the young king have the strength and wisdom to do the same?

Huldah had lived in the same house for many years. She was the wife of Shallum, the keeper of the king's wardrobe, and she was famous for the fineness of her weaving. Her cloth had been used to dress kings and priests. Many women came to her home, asking her to teach them her skills, and secretly she also taught them their history and their proud and godly heritage.

'When you have woven a whole length of cloth, then perhaps you will also have learned a small part of the Law,' she would say to them. 'A tiny bit of knowledge grows like a child. Some day you will read the Torah for yourselves and will teach it to your children.'

Two years later, when Josiah was ten years old, his mother summoned Huldah to the palace. 'I wonder why the Queen Mother wishes to speak with me,' she thought. When she reached the palace, she was shown into Jedidah's rooms. The young mother smiled. 'Please sit down, Huldah,' she said, pointing to a chair beside a table laden with fruit and sweets.

Huldah felt anxious. What did the Queen Mother want?

Jedidah dismissed her servants and then turned to her guest. 'I have asked you to come because I have been told by Hilkiah, the High Priest, that you are a wise woman.' She offered Huldah a tray of fruit. 'I want Josiah to be taught our true heritage. His father and grandfather worshipped false gods, and led the people of Judah astray. The people do not know about our history, or about the Lord. Josiah, too, is ignorant.'

'What do you want me to do, Jedidah?' Huldah asked, uneasily. She wanted to know exactly what the Queen Mother required of her.

'I want you to teach Josiah the Law of the Torah.'

'Should not Hilkiah, the High Priest, do that?'

'Hilkiah teaches with his head, but you teach with your heart.'

Huldah laughed. 'I am an old woman, a weaver of cloth. I am not a teacher. True, I teach the women of Jerusalem how to use a loom, how to choose proper yarn.'

'I have heard that you teach the women more than just weaving,' Jedidah replied.

'What have you heard?'

'That you teach them the history of our people and the importance of worshipping only one God.'

Huldah sat very still; she wasn't sure whether it was safe for her to do as Jedidah asked. 'Give me time to think about your request.'

'No!' Josiah's mother rose from her chair. 'No, Huldah, you need not hesitate. This is purely between you and me. My son is now ten years old, and soon he will no longer be a child. You will not only be teaching Josiah, but you will be teaching the King of Judah, and through him an entire people.'

'Are you ordering me to do this? Is this a command?' Huldah asked.

Jedidah took Huldah's hand. 'It is a mother's request to a wise woman.'

'I cannot refuse a mother's request,' Huldah answered softly. 'But where shall I teach him?'

'Not in the palace. There are too many ears in the walls and too many eyes in the windows.'

'I teach weaving in my home. Perhaps Josiah could come with you while I give you lessons?'

Surprised at this idea, Jedidah laughed. 'That's a good suggestion. Yes, I will learn to weave and young Josiah will learn the way of our Lord at the same time.'

On the appointed day, the king and his mother stood at the gate to Huldah's home. The guards were ordered to wait outside the door while Huldah took her visitors through the house and out into the garden. There the loom hung ready from the tree. The warp had been stretched over two heavy poles, and Huldah had started the weaving. Two stools stood in front of the loom for Jedidah and Josiah to sit upon.

Huldah stood behind them. 'We shall use linen thread as was used for the clothes of the High Priest Aaron and his sons. And, as the Lord commanded, we shall weave the colours blue, purple and scarlet.'

'What do you mean — as the Lord commanded?' asked Josiah.

'It is written in our Book of Laws that the Lord appeared in a pillar of smoke by day and a pillar of flame by night and gave Moses the Law to pass on to our people.'

'I am now the King of Judah,' said Josiah. 'I should like to know what the Lord said.'

Jedidah rested her hand on her son's arm. 'If you listen carefully to your heart, my son, you will surely hear the words of the Lord.'

As Josiah grew, he listened to the teachings of Moses and he ordered the holy Temple to be rebuilt. While his workmen were engaged in repairing an outer wall, they found a scroll of ancient parchment. The workmen were afraid, and carried it carefully to the High Priest, Hilkiah.

The High Priest held the ancient scroll with awe, and started to unroll it. It was still readable, and Hilkiah grew cold with fear as he realised what he was holding. 'This is the word of the Lord as it was given to Moses.' He called to the scribe, Shaphan, to witness what had been found. Despite his position as High Priest, Hilkiah did not want to be held responsible for the discovery of the scroll. 'Take this to the king, Shaphan, and read it aloud to him.'

The scribe's heart pounded as he ran to the palace. He bowed low and presented the Holy Scroll to the king.

'What is this?' asked Josiah.

'It is a long lost scroll, Your Highness. The workmen found it concealed in the wall of the Temple. Hilkiah thinks it was written by Moses.'

'A holy scroll of Moses!' Josiah went pale. 'Has it been read by anyone?'

'Only by Hilkiah and me, Your Highness.'

'Leave the scroll with me.' Josiah dismissed the scribe. Then he unrolled the scroll and started to read it. He read,

'Behold, I will bring evil upon this place, and upon the inhabitants thereof, even all the words of the book which the King of Judah hath read; because they have forsaken Me and have offered unto other gods, that they might provoke Me with all the work of their hands; therefore My wrath shall be kindled against this place, and it shall not be quenched.'

Josiah was afraid. 'What does this mean?' he cried out, and in his terror he tore his clothes. 'It is the wrath of God!' Bursting into tears, he raced through the palace to his mother's quarters.

'Mother,' he sobbed. 'Look at this scroll. I am afraid of the words written on it.'

'Where did it come from?' Jedidah asked.

'The workmen rebuilding the Temple found it hidden in a wall. Hilkiah thinks it was put here when the temple was first built. He sent Shaphan to me with it. I think he was afraid to come himself.'

'What was he afraid of?'

'When I unrolled the scroll I found words which frightened me, too.' Josiah searched through the scroll until he found the passage he had read before. 'Here, Mother. Read it for yourself.'

Jedidah turned pale as she read the words he pointed to. It was as if Moses had forseen the evil reigns of Manasseh and Amon. 'Let's go to Huldah, the prophetess, and ask her what to do,' she said.

Together, Jedidah and Josiah hurried to Huldah's house. When she saw how distressed they were she quickly beckoned them inside.

Jedidah did not know how to explain their anguish to Huldah, but she

guessed from their tear-stained faces that it had something to do with the scroll which Josiah was still clutching. He explained where it had been found, and that the High Priest had been too afraid to bring it to him. Josiah unrolled the scroll and showed Huldah the passage which had terrified him. She read it silently, and then she took Josiah's hand in hers. 'Listen to me,' she said, closing her eyes and feeling a guiding voice speaking from deep inside herself. 'Because you cried and tore your clothes, you humbled yourself before the Lord. He has heard your weeping, and He knows of your sorrow and repentance.' She opened her eyes. 'Look at me, Josiah. The punishment will not come to pass in your lifetime, and you will live in peace.'

Jedidah and Josiah clung to each other and wept, but this time they were tears of relief.

'Now, Josiah,' Huldah said softly. 'Leave the scroll and ask Hilkiah and Shaphan to come to me.'

When the High Priest and the scribe arrived, Huldah told them that Josiah had come to her for help because they had been too cowardly themselves to comfort him. 'How did you manage to console him?' Hilkiah asked sulkily.

Huldah controlled her anger, and said quietly, 'Because Josiah humbled himself before the Lord, He vowed that he would live in peace. Josiah will not live to see evil brought on this place.'

When Hilkiah returned to the palace, the king requested him to call all the people together at the House of the Lord. Josiah read aloud from the scroll and then he and all the people made a covenant, a promise, to the Lord that they would keep His commandments and His laws.

'Above all,' vowed Josiah, 'I will confirm the words of this covenant with all my heart and with all my soul, for the words in this Holy Scroll are the words of Moses himself.'

With one voice, the people agreed.

From her home in the hills, Huldah saw the people enter the Temple, and Jedidah's words came back to her, '…you will not only be teaching Josiah, but you will be teaching the King of Judah, and through him an entire people.'

Huldah, the prophetess, lived for many more years, and so she witnessed the king and his people dwelling in peace and happiness all their days.

THE BIBLE, THE APOCRYPHA AND JUDITH

*O*ver the course of history, the Jews developed a library of sacred writings —
history, poetry and fiction. Some groups considered certain books to be more
important than others. Originally, all of the writings were considered holy but,
as time passed, it became clear that the literature had to be divided, to separate
the word inspired by God from other texts. The Bible, as we know it now, was
not standardised until about AD 100 . The rabbis at that time read the whole of
Jewish literature and then had to decide which works were the word of God
and which ones were not. Those books that were included became the Bible,
while those that were left out became known as the Apocrypha.

~

The story of Judith was not included in the Bible and is therefore part of
the Apocrypha. Today, scholars point out names and dates in
the story which are inconsistent.

~

The story is set around 600 BC, at a time which saw waves of powerful armies
from Babylonia sweeping through the land of Israel. Who among the Israelites
was strong enough to resist? Certainly, it was unusual for a woman to save a
city, which is why the story of Judith is one of the best-known in the Apocrypha.

~

The Bible tells us that Judith was among the most beautiful of women. By
entering the enemy camp, she and her handmaid were risking physical assault
by the Babylonian soldiers. The two women must have trembled in fear as they
were first apprehended. They must have quaked as their plan unfolded in
the very tent of the Babylonian general. But courage is the overcoming of
fear and the two brave women prevailed.

~

Historically, the Babylonians were eventually the victors. In 586 BC they
conquered the Jews, destroyed Solomon's Temple and took many Jews back
to Babylon as slaves.

JUDITH

It was exceedingly hot in the town of Bethulia, which lay three days' travel north of Jerusalem. Judith peered out from the shaded bower of grapevines. In the distance she could see her husband overseeing the workers binding sheaves of wheat.

'It is midday,' she murmured. 'I must call my husband. It is too hot to be in the full sun.'

She stepped from the shade. 'Manasseh!' she called. He did not turn to her voice. 'Manasseh!' she shouted again, and waved her arms. This time he turned, waved and walked towards her. Suddenly he disappeared from view. It was as if the wheat had swallowed him.

Judith ran to the place where she had last seen her husband. When she reached him, he lay crumpled on the ground. She bent to touch his face; he did not seem to be alive. 'Bring your master to the house,' she ordered the workers. They carried him in and laid him on his bed in a cool room.

For ten days Manasseh lay still, his eyes closed. Judith bathed him with spring water to cool his burning flesh. On the eleventh day she held his lifeless hand and sobbed. The elders of Bethulia said prayers for the dead while Manasseh's body was carried to rest with his ancestors.

Now, as a widow, Judith dressed in sackcloth and bound her hair about her head. She could not bear to use the rooms where she and Manasseh had

been so happy, so she had a tent erected on the roof of her house. She and her maidservant, Meshara, slept there.

Manasseh had provided well for his wife. Judith was left a wealthy woman, with workers, livestock and fields. She maintained these carefully, and none of the men who worked for her, or their families, spoke ill of her. Everyone agreed that she was kind and honest.

About this time, Nebuchadnezzar, the king of Assyria, left his capital at Nineveh, and embarked on a bitter war with the Midianites. He sent his general, Holofernes, to capture all the land south of Nineveh, right down to Jerusalem.

Judith and her neighbours were frightened when they heard of the danger. One young woman spoke softly, 'It is said that the Assyrians have twenty thousand soldiers.'

An older woman nodded. 'Bethulia is small. Our city wall will not withstand such a force.'

'Bethulia is a long way south of Nineveh,' Judith reassured her.

'What if they cut us off from our water source?' worried another.

'Uzziah, our magistrate, will protect us. His name means "God is my strength". He will look after us. And if we show fear, it will make us weak,' Judith answered. 'We must be strong and put our faith in the Lord.'

Two days later, after the Sabbath, Uzziah called all the men of Bethulia to a meeting in the town square. Judith stood on the outskirts of the crowd. As a woman, it was not proper for her to stand with the men.

'Nebuchadnezzar is threatening us,' said Uzziah. 'He demands that all the lands west of Persia surrender to him.'

Voices called out in protest. Judith clenched her fists as Uzziah continued bitterly, 'He threatens to destroy all nations who do not accede to his demands. We must arm ourselves, and we must store food and water.'

Judith stared at this man on whom the people of Bethulia were depending. 'And what of God?' she said to herself. 'Uzziah is putting his faith into arms. I am afraid he has forgotten how to pray.' She was very troubled as she made her way home.

A few days later Uzziah called another meeting. Word had come that the

Assyrians had reached the sea. Under the command of Holofernes, they had captured and plundered the cities of Tyre and Ascalon. Villages were levelled, crops burned, sanctuaries destroyed and the people slaughtered. Holofernes demanded that all should worship Nebuchadnezzar, not only as a king but also as a god.

'Our water supply is threatened. There has been no rain,' Uzziah went on. 'We must save as much water as we can. If God sends us no rain within five days, we are lost.'

Judith pushed her way through the frightened crowd until she stood face to face with Uzziah. 'What you have said to the people is not right, Uzziah. You talk of us surrendering if the Lord does not send rain.'

'We have only enough water to last five days,' Uzziah repeated. 'The enemy is camped less than a day away.' He stared at Judith. 'You are a god-fearing woman. Pray for us. Perhaps the Lord will send us rain.'

'Are you putting our Lord to the test, Uzziah?' Judith demanded, and then turned away. Talking was no use — now was the time for action, but what action could she take?

Back in her rooftop tent, Judith meditated and then prayed. 'O Lord, help me. Help me to deliver my people from harm.' She held her arms tightly round her body as though for protection. Should it be up to a woman to save her neighbours?

She stood with her eyes closed. A plan, she must have a plan. As night fell, she said her prayers, and then turned her eyes to the heavens. 'Holofernes is a man. I will approach him as a woman.'

As dawn broke, Judith stood at Uzziah's door. He opened it at her knock and she said, 'Uzziah, I have a plan which, should it succeed, will save Bethulia and Jerusalem.'

Uzziah looked astonished. 'Judith, what do you mean?'

'Stand at the town gate tonight. I will go out with my maid. Do not try to find out what I will be doing, and in five days, God willing, I will return and tell you where I have been.'

Uzziah stared at her, then he looked up to the heavens and his lips moved in prayer. 'I pray for your safety, Judith.'

Back home, Judith called Meshara. 'Do as I say. In a fine cloth, wrap all the dishes we will need for five days. Take a skin of wine, a flask of oil, a bag filled with roasted grain, a string of figs and plenty of bread. Put all our food in a strong, tightly woven bag.' Then she retired to the tent on the roof and prayed again, 'O Lord, hear the prayer of a widow. Make my hands strong to do what I plan.'

She bathed, anointed herself with scented oils, unbraided her hair and combed it straight and long. She dressed in her best clothes, clothes she had last worn when Manasseh was alive. She put on bracelets, rings, ear-rings, anklets and sandals. Her aim was to entice any man who saw her. She was ready to face Bethulia's enemy.

The full moon was shining as Judith and Meshara walked to the town gate where Uzziah was waiting. He was stunned by the transformation from the widow dressed in black to this elegant and beautiful woman. 'May the Lord grant you favour, Judith, and may He help you to fulfil your mission.'

He ordered the gates to be opened and Judith and Meshara walked out of the town.

'My lady, where are we going?' Meshara whispered.

'Have no fear,' answered Judith. 'The Lord will show us the way.'

The two women reached the valley and started walking north. They were getting tired when they were stopped by a shout. They stood still and Meshara moved closer to her mistress. 'Be brave,' Judith whispered. 'Stand tall. Hold your head high.'

They were approached by Assyrian soldiers. 'Two women walking alone at night! Who are you and where are you going?'

Judith stood proudly. She looked like a princess. 'I am on my way to meet General Holofernes.'

'A beautiful woman walking alone to meet our leader?' asked one man, while the others burst into laughter.

'I am a daughter of the Hebrews,' Judith stated. 'I am fleeing, for it is known that General Holofernes will soon capture Jerusalem. I have a plan which the general may find helpful to him and his men.'

'We will take you to our general.' As they walked through the camp, word spread of a beautiful woman who had come to see the general. Soon hundreds of soldiers were following her. Judith and Meshara waited outside Holofernes' tent while their guides went in. As soon as he was told, Holofernes stopped his work and rose to meet her. He was startled by her beauty.

Judith bowed, and then knelt on the carpet in respect.

'Arise, woman.' He smiled. 'My men tell me that you are a Hebrew. Why have you come to the camp of your enemy?'

Judith faced him. Her heart beat quickly. 'Accept the words of your servant,' she said, and again bowed low. 'My people have angered our God. Our water will soon be gone and our food exhausted.' Her eyes never left his face. This was what she wanted; a woman talking to a man. 'The Lord will cause the Hebrews to be handed over to you.'

The general smiled. 'You are not only beautiful, you are wise. If you are right, you will live in the palace of King Nebuchadnezzar and your name will be known throughout the kingdom.'

'I will stay with you, my lord, but my maid and I need our own tent. And you must allow us to go down into the valley and pray before daybreak. When God tells me it is the right moment, I will lead you through Judah, and Jerusalem will be yours.'

Holofernes agreed, and then ordered a table of delicacies to be placed in front of Judith.

'I thank you, my lord,' and again she bowed low, 'but it is against my religion to eat your food. I have brought my own food with me.'

'What will you do when your food is gone?'

'I will not go hungry,' she smiled. 'And now, sir, it is late and I am tired.'

The two women retired to their tent and slept until daybreak. Then Judith sent word to Holofernes that she wanted to go down to the valley and bathe in the spring waters. She was not to be followed. She was not to be watched.

At daybreak every morning after that, she and Meshara left their tent and went down to bathe. There, in private, she was able to pray for guidance.

On the fourth night, Holofernes ordered a banquet to be prepared in Judith's honour. His servant was sent to invite her. 'General Holofernes wishes you to drink wine with him. He would like to celebrate your desire to lead him to victory against the Hebrews.'

'Whatever pleases your leader, I will do,' she replied, and going back into her tent she began to get ready. She anointed herself with perfumed oils and decked herself with bracelets, rings, ear-rings, anklets and sandals. She told Meshara, 'Whatever happens, dear friend, you must wait outside Holofernes' tent. When I call, be ready to go down to the valley once more.'

The general's tent had been made ready for the banquet. Over his bed stretched a canopy of purple and gold, woven with emeralds. On a round table, fine food was prepared and two delicate glasses stood ready, filled with wine. There was a decanter of wine to refill them. Sheepskins lay on the carpets for Judith's comfort. When Judith entered, her long hair shining and her gown flowing, she looked like a queen. Holofernes raised his glass. 'I drink to your beauty and to a joyful evening.'

'I am glad to join you, my lord,' Judith said, 'but I can only eat and drink what my maid has prepared.'

'As you wish,' Holofernes replied, surprised, but he ordered his servants to bring two more decanters of wine.

Judith entertained him with stories of the Hebrews, stories of their victories and their defeats. Soon the general dismissed his attendants and his guards. As the evening wore on, Judith steadily refilled his glass and Holofernes became more and more drunk. When the third decanter was finished, he staggered to his bed in a drunken stupor and was soon sound asleep.

Judith stood by the bed and prayed. 'O Lord, look upon the work of my hands as the means of freedom for Bethulia and Jerusalem. Now I must destroy the enemy who would destroy us.' She lifted the sword which hung from the bedpost and held it high. 'O Lord, give me strength,' she whispered. With that, she struck his neck twice and severed his head. She pushed his body off the bed and pulled down the canopy to cover the body. She shivered. 'Dear God, forgive me.'

Judith opened the tent door and whispered for Meshara to put the head in her empty food basket. Horrified, Meshara obeyed.

Closing the tent, the two women walked down to the valley, climbed the mountain to Bethulia and came to its gates. Dawn was breaking when she called out, 'Open! Open the gates!'

'Judith is back!' Uzziah shouted and the gate was opened.

As Judith stepped through the gate she sang out, 'Our enemy has been destroyed!' She reached into the basket and held Holofernes' head high in the air. 'Here is the head of our enemy. The Lord caused him to be struck down by a woman's hand!'

Judith smiled at Uzziah. 'As Meshara is my witness, he did not defile nor shame me. I committed no sin.'

Uzziah placed the head on a pole, high above the city wall for everyone to see. He turned to Judith. 'You are truly blessed. You risked your life to save us all.'

When Holofernes' servants found his headless body, they were terrified. Their general had been killed by a woman! They ran through the camp screaming the news. Without a leader, the soldiers panicked and ran in every direction. They were easily defeated by the Israelite army.

Judith was honoured throughout the land. The story of her courage and bravery was told over and over again. It is said that she lived to be a hundred and five years old, at which time Meshara was granted her freedom. While Judith lived, no one ever spread terror again among the people of Israel, nor for a long time after her death.

THE MESSAGE OF ESTHER

The story of Esther, which takes place in about 470 BC, tells of a conspiracy. All the Jews in the land of Persia were to be killed. Esther is told by her uncle, 'Do not think that concealing your identity will save you.' This message has been true for the Jews many times in their history.

~

When King Ferdinand and Queen Isabella came to power in Spain in AD 1492, the Inquisition began. Jews were offered a choice — convert to Catholicism, leave the country or be killed. Some Jews tried to hide their identity. If they were discovered, they were burnt at the stake.

~

In Russia, the tsars periodically initiated a series of pogroms in which Jewish settlements were raided and Jews killed. You may have seen part of this story in the musical production of Fiddler on the Roof.

~

In Nazi Germany, Hitler and his government embarked on a plan to eliminate all Jews from the countries they conquered. As in the days of Esther, trying to conceal the fact that one was a Jew was no protection.

~

The story of Esther, however, is a story of triumph, for Esther did not keep secret her identity as a Jew and by her actions many lives were saved. Today the holiday of Purim celebrates Esther. Little girls dress up as Queen Esther in all her royal finery and many people masquerade. Everyone feasts on Haman's hats, which are pastries filled with fruit or poppy seeds, also called 'hamantaschen'. An important aspect of the Purim celebration is the collection and distribution of food to poor people, just as the poor of the city of Shushan shared in Esther's wedding feast all those years ago.

ESTHER

'I am alone,' five-year-old Hadassah sobbed at her father's funeral. Her mother was dead, and now her father was too. She shivered as the chilling rain fell on her bowed head.

'It is said that raindrops are angels' tears.'

Hadassah barely heard the soft voice, nor felt the hand upon her shoulder. She looked up and recognised her father's brother. 'Uncle Mordecai?'

'I am your family,' he said kindly. 'You will come and live with me, Hadassah. My wife and I will look after you.'

Hadassah nodded and watched as wet soil covered her father's grave and the last prayers were chanted. She took her uncle's hand as they walked from the cemetery. 'If I live with you, Uncle Mordecai, where will that be?'

'In Shushan.'

'Where the king lives?'

'Yes.'

'It is far away.'

'Yes. My horse will carry us there.'

Night had fallen by the time they reached Mordecai's home. His wife took the sleepy child in her arms, carried her into the house and put her to bed.

At breakfast, Hadassah looked at her aunt and uncle, who smiled at her.

'I will never smile again,' she whispered, but she was wrong. In this warm

81

and loving family, she found happiness, and she grew to be a beautiful young woman — beautiful not only in her face, but in her manner and her speech. She studied with her uncle and aunt and learned the mitzvot, or holy commandments, that all Jewish women need to perform.

One morning, as Hadassah stood in the doorway of her home, she saw people rushing towards the palace shouting, 'Vashti! Vashti!'

She called out, 'Uncle, come quickly! What is happening?'

'A terrible thing,' Mordecai answered, shaking his head. 'Queen Vashti has refused to obey King Ahashverosh's wishes.'

'The queen has refused the king?' Hadassah looked up at her uncle. 'What will happen to her?'

'That will depend on the king's advisors.'

'Cannot the king decide for himself?'

'A wise man knows he cannot know everything. He will listen to what his advisors say, and then he will think for himself.'

By the third day, a large crowd had gathered outside the palace. Hadassah stayed at home. She and Aunt Haninah peered at the people through the partly closed window. There was a sudden roar from the crowd and, excitedly, they pushed the window wide open. One of the king's advisors appeared at the King's Gate. Dressed in royal robes, he proclaimed, 'The order of King Ahashverosh has not been obeyed by Queen Vashti. A wife must always obey her husband. That is the law!'

There was a roar of approval from the crowd of men gathered outside the palace as the king's advisor continued: 'Vashti will be hanged by the neck until she is dead.' There was another roar of approval.

Hadassah turned to Haninah. 'Death for disobeying the king!' she gasped. 'How terrible!'

'It is a lesson for all the women of Shushan and of the entire kingdom of Persia,' her aunt whispered.

After Vashti was hanged, a feeling of melancholy settled on the city. While the men approved of the king's action, the women were afraid. Then Haman, the Chief of the King's Council, decided something must be done to lift the spirits of the king and the citizens. 'Your Majesty,' he said. 'I propose to find a woman more beautiful than Vashti. Issue a royal decree that all the most beautiful girls in Persia be summoned to Shushan. Then you, King Ahashverosh, the ruler of all Persia, will be able to choose the most beautiful girl in the whole world to be your wife.'

The king agreed, and Haman sent out notices from India to Ethiopia that the most beautiful girls in all of Babylonia should come to Shushan so that the king might choose his next wife.

Mordecai spoke to his wife and his niece. 'The king is looking for a beautiful girl to replace his queen. Hadassah, you are sixteen years old, and a woman. I am afraid for you.'

'But I am Jewish,' Hadassah answered. 'A Jew would not be chosen to be queen.'

'But the king's advisors know that there is a girl of extraordinary beauty living in Shushan,' said Mordecai. 'I think that you are that girl.'

Hadassah was hidden away and not allowed out of the house. Then a new decree was issued: anyone found hiding a beautiful girl would be put to death. Haninah was frightened. 'Mordecai, if we continue to hide Hadassah, we will surely be killed. And if it is known that she is a Jew, then she will be killed as well.'

'My dearest Aunt,' said Hadassah. 'Let me go out into the main square where all the girls of Shushan meet. If I am chosen, God will watch over me. If I am not chosen,' she smiled, 'I will return home to you.'

'Before you go,' Mordecai said, 'your name must be changed. Hadassah is a Hebrew name. You will have to hide your true identity if you are chosen, for Haman, the leader of the King's Council, hates Jews. He would willingly have you murdered. Before you leave, I shall give you the name of Esther, for it means "to conceal".'

'Very well, Uncle,' Esther said sadly. 'My true name, my true religion and my true self will all be hidden.'

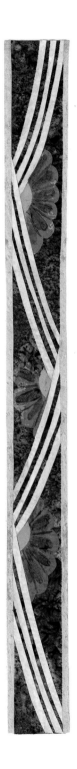

In the main square there was an air of excitement. Would someone be chosen today? Esther kept her head down and her face hidden behind a soft veil. As she walked among the crowd, she was afraid. 'What am I doing here?' she thought. 'These innocent women are offering themselves as if they were items for sale.' She shivered, and bent her head even lower. 'A woman is not a water-jug, to be bought at the market.'

'Ho!' called one of the king's guards. 'Why do you hide your face, my pretty?' He reached for her veil and Esther's beauty was revealed. He stared, and then spoke softly. 'You are the girl for whom we have been searching. Come with me.'

As Esther followed him she prayed for her safety. She was taken to Hagai, the Chief Harem-keeper. 'You are, indeed, beautiful,' he said, smiling. 'And your beauty will crown you Queen of Persia. What is your name?'

She hesitated. 'I am called Esther.'

She was led away to the women's quarters. 'These are the best rooms,' said Hagai. 'I will send four women to wait on you.'

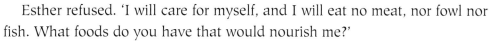

Esther refused. 'I will care for myself, and I will eat no meat, nor fowl nor fish. What foods do you have that would nourish me?'

'We grow lovely vegetables in the king's garden.'

Esther laughed. 'I would be delighted to eat the king's vegetables.'

Hagai took special care of Esther, for he believed that she would be chosen to be his queen.

For a year, all the beautiful maidens waiting in the king's palace were made ready to meet him. They were taught how to look after themselves and instructed in the use of myrrh oil, perfumes and cosmetics. When it was the right time, they were each presented in turn to the king. Those he approved of were sent to the harem. The others were sent home, shamed and in tears. When she saw the weeping girls leaving the palace Esther thought, 'You fortunate girls. I would not cry, I would sing all the way home!'

When it was Esther's turn to go before King Ahashverosh, she refused the glittering gowns, costly cosmetics and perfumes offered to her by Hagai. 'I will be myself,' she said.

The king compared each maiden that came before him with a picture of Vashti which hung in the throne room. When Esther approached, simply dressed in the clothes of an ordinary Persian woman, her face scrubbed clean and her long hair hanging straight down her back, he gasped. He had never seen unadorned, natural beauty before. She was splendid in her purity. Esther, indeed, would be his queen. He called to his servants to remove Vashti's picture and announced that a painting of Esther would hang in its place.

'Esther, I have chosen you to be my wife and my queen.'

Esther bowed low to hide her tears.

'You will be queen of the great Persian Empire,' the king announced, placing a crown on her head. 'We will have a great feast to celebrate our marriage. All of Shushan will be invited.'

'My noble king,' said Esther. 'There are many poor people in Shushan.' She paused, waiting for his reaction. When he said nothing, she continued, 'If you wish to declare a true holiday in my honour, you should send baskets of food to every home. That way, all of Shushan would be able to celebrate our wedding.'

The king was as impressed by her wisdom as by her beauty. 'And you, my queen, may invite whoever you wish.'

'Alas, Your Majesty, I am an orphan. My mother died in childbirth and my father when I was a small child.'

The king accepted her word and so Esther was able to conceal from him the fact that she was Jewish. As time passed, King Ahashverosh came to love Esther as his true wife. He shared his problems with her and she suggested ways in which he could help his people and make their lives easier. One day, he told her how much he disliked having to sit at the King's Gate for hours every day, sitting in judgement on the problems and petty complaints of his people. Esther had a suggestion.

'My noble King,' she said, taking his hand. 'I have heard of wise men from a nation known as Israel. They have a reputation for clarity of thought and sound advice.'

'Are there such men here in Babylonia?'

'Yes, Your Majesty, there are. I have heard of a descendant of King Saul who lives here in Shushan. His name is Mordecai and he is reputed to have one of the best minds in the kingdom.'

'I should like to meet this man. If he is as wise as you claim, I will appoint him one of my royal advisors, and he can sit as judge at the King's Gate.'

And so it was that Mordecai took the king's place at the gate, and sat in judgement on the problems which the citizens of Shushan brought before him. Esther watched him through a small window but she knew she could not approach him or acknowledge him as her uncle.

One day, however, she became aware that he wanted to speak to her. Opening a door, she stepped out into the small square and at once Mordecai rushed towards her. 'Esther,' he said. 'I have overheard something terrible. Two of the king's servants are planning to kill him. You must tell the king.'

Esther hurried to the throne room, waited until she was recognised and then approached the king. 'Your Majesty, your new judge at the King's Gate has come to me with shocking information. He has heard two of your servants plotting to kill you.'

'What?' shouted the king. 'Kill me?' He stood with his fists clenched, his face red with fury. 'Their names! What are their names?'

'Bigthan and Teresh.'

'They shall be hanged for treason.'

Bigthan and Teresh were friends of Haman, the Chief of the King's Council. When he heard of their arrest, he rushed to the palace and Esther listened as he argued unsuccessfully for their release. 'Why is he defending two men who plotted to kill the king?' she wondered.

The royal scribes were ordered to record the incident in the palace archives. Esther reminded them to note that Mordecai deserved a reward for saving the king's life, but days passed and no reward was given. Instead, Haman cursed Mordecai every time he saw him at the King's Gate. Then he began to act as if he was of royal blood himself. He wore royal robes and was driven in a special chariot. When he rode through the streets, a crier would run beside his chariot and call out, 'Behold! Haman, Head of Council! All kneel down!'

When Esther heard this she laughed. 'Uncle Mordecai will never kneel down before this or any man.' She was right. Not only did he refuse to bow down, he would not stand up, either. He looked Haman full in the face every time he passed by. Haman was furious, and Esther was afraid that one day he would try to kill Mordecai.

One of the king's servants asked Mordecai why he did not bow down.

'Haman is merely a mortal, just as I am,' he replied. 'As a Jew, I bow down only to God.'

When the servant repeated to Haman what Mordecai had said, he was even angrier. He vowed he would kill Mordecai and all his fellow Jews. He must think of a way of doing it discreetly.

One of Esther's servants reported seeing Haman coming from the Court Astrologers, a pair of dice in his hands. 'I cannot leave the palace to find out what is going on,' Esther said to her. 'You must be my eyes and ears and find out what Haman is doing.'

The servant watched as Haman threw the dice time after time. Finally he stood up and smiled. 'It will be the thirteenth day of the month of Adar. Again and again the dice confirm it. It will be the death of the Jews!' He threw back his head and laughed loudly. 'Death to all of them!'

The servant ran to tell the queen what she had witnessed, just as Haman hurried to the palace to stand before the king. 'There is a group of people

living in this kingdom, my lord, who do not obey my laws, and so do not obey your laws. They live by their own rules — this is not right. If a citizen does not obey the law of the land, he should be punished. Let an order be given to destroy them and I will pay ten thousand talents of silver to the royal treasury.'

'I do not need your money,' said King Ahashverosh. 'But do what you wish with these people.'

Haman sent out proclamations that very day. Runners carried the edicts all over the king's lands. 'Destroy all the Jews, young and old, on the thirteenth day of the month of Adar. Seal up your city gates and do not allow any of them to escape.'

When Mordecai heard the decree he put on sackcloth and ashes. At his post at the King's Gate he screamed out, 'Haman has vowed to kill us all!' He continued to shout until he attracted the attention of Esther's servants, who quickly informed the queen. As soon as she heard, Esther sent her manservant Hathach to find out what was happening. Mordecai gave him a copy of the proclamation. 'Tell Queen Esther that she must go to the king and beg for mercy,' he told him.

'I cannot do that,' Esther said. 'Anyone who dares to go into the inner court of the king without being summoned is put to death.' She paced back and forth. 'I will be killed unless the king stretches out the golden sceptre to indicate that I may live.' Then she realised that if she wanted to save her people, she would have to risk her life. Quietly Esther bathed. She combed her long shining hair, put on a dress of the finest silk, adorned herself with her richest jewels, placed golden slippers on her feet and her royal crown on her head. Her heart was pounding. 'Be not far from me, dear God, for trouble is near,' she prayed. She waited at the entrance to the throne room.

The king, sitting on his throne, thought only of how beautiful she was. He stretched forth his golden sceptre in approval. Slowly, Esther approached and touched the tip of the sceptre.

'What is it, my queen?'

'If it pleases the king, let him and Haman come to a feast which I have prepared.' She trembled. Did the king suspect that she was Jewish?

'This very day, my queen?'

'This very day.'

King Ahashverosh ordered Haman to join him while he dined with the queen. As they ate, the king asked Esther, 'What is it you want, my queen? Whatever it is, I shall grant it.'

'I have only one request,' she replied. 'That you and Haman come to eat at my table again tomorrow. Then I will present the king with the gift he so desires. I will reveal my true identity.'

That night the king could not sleep. As he tossed and turned, he worried about his queen. Why had she risked her life to come to him? What did she really want? Then his thoughts turned to Mordecai. He was sure that there was something he should have remembered about him. He called a servant to bring him the Book of Records from the royal archives. After reading for an hour he found what he was looking for. 'Mordecai once saved my life,' he said to the servant. 'What reward and honour has been given to him?'

'Nothing, my lord. Nothing has been done for Mordecai.'

The next morning, as the king sat on his throne, it was announced that Haman was awaiting audience with him. 'Let him come in,' ordered the king.

As Haman stood before him, the king said, 'You are the Head of my Council. I have a problem which I would like you to solve for me. What should be done for a man whom the king wishes to honour?'

Haman, assuming that the king was referring to him, said, 'Let the man be dressed in the king's royal robes. Give him the king's favourite horse and lead him through the streets calling out, "Thus it shall be done for the man whom the king wishes to honour."'

'Excellent,' King Ahashverosh smiled. 'Take the robes and the horse, Haman. Go to the King's Gate and honour Mordecai, the Jew, who sits there.'

So Haman was forced to walk to the King's Gate, carrying the royal robes, to where his bitter enemy, Mordecai, still sat wearing sackcloth and ashes. Gloomily, he gave Mordecai the king's message. While Mordecai went home to bathe and to dress in the royal robes, Haman sent for the king's favourite horse. Then he had to lead the man he loathed through the streets of Shushan. A crowd followed singing Mordecai's praises. As they passed under the windows of Haman's house, his daughter looked out. Mistaking the man on the horse for her father, she assumed that the dejected figure leading him must be Mordecai and emptied a pot of rubbish over his head. When Haman looked up and saw that it was his own daughter who had humiliated him, he hung his head even lower.

When they arrived back at the King's Gate, Haman hurried home. He was still bidden to dine with the king and queen again that night and he needed time to prepare himself.

That evening, the king looked lovingly at Esther, and asked her, 'Now tell me what it is that you want and it shall be given to you.'

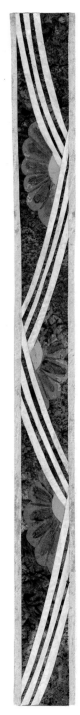

'I am of royal blood, a descendant of King Saul of Israel.' Esther spoke clearly, her head held high. 'My enemy wants to kill me and all my people.' She looked into the king's eyes. 'The first thing I request, most noble King, is that you grant me my life.'

The king was astonished. 'My queen, of course, I grant you your life. I love you. I want you to live.'

'If you wish to give me a gift, my royal King, do not harm my people. Spare us from our cruel and wicked enemy.'

'Who is it?' he shouted. 'Who is your enemy, my queen?'

Esther pointed to Haman. 'This man is my enemy. He is your enemy, also, for he wants to kill you and take your kingdom. My uncle, Mordecai, heard this with his own ears.'

The king summoned Mordecai into his presence at once and questioned him closely.

'All the charges against the Jews are false,' Mordecai said. 'King Ahashverosh, you must act quickly to cancel the decrees of Haman, or all the Jews in your kingdom will die.'

'Take your enemy and mine to the gallows he prepared for you and all your people. Hang him at once,' the king said to Mordecai. A hood was placed over Haman's head and he was led out. When Mordecai returned, the king gave him his royal signet ring. 'Write to all the governors of the lands from Ethiopia to India retracting Haman's evil decree. Let it be known that King Ahashverosh wishes his people and the Jews to live together in peace. Seal the document with my ring, stamped in wax. With my seal, this decree cannot be broken.'

Mordecai sent messengers, riding fast horses, to all the corners of the land carrying the king's decree. Joy rang out through Shushan. Mordecai was praised as a hero as he walked through the streets wearing royal robes of purple and white. The Jews gathered on the thirteenth and fourteenth days of Adar, and celebrated. They called their celebration Purim, vowing that these days of joy and peace should be remembered and kept for each generation in every family and in every land.

BIBLIOGRAPHY

MIRIAM

Asimov, Isaac, *Asimov's Guide to the Bible*, Doubleday & Co., New York, 1968, pp. 129, 168.

Cohen, A. (ed.), *The Soncino Chumash*, The Soncino Press, London, 1966, pp. 321–5ff., 549–50ff.

Cohen, Mortimer J., *Pathways through the Bible*, second edition, The Jewish Publication Society of America, Philadelphia, 1960–65, pp. 551ff.

Epstein, Rabbi I. (trans. and ed.), *The Babylonian Talmud: Seder Mo'ed*, The Soncino Press, London, 1938, p. 164.

Hertz, Dr J. H. (ed.), *The Pentateuch and Haftorahs*, The Soncino Press, London, 1966, pp. 209–10, 273, 618–19, 655–6.

The Holy Scriptures, The Jewish Publication Society of America, Philadelphia, 1955, pp. 73, 95, 97, 195.

The Jewish Encyclopedia, 12 vols, KTAV Publishing House, New York, 1901, vol. 8, pp. 608–9.

Landman, Isaac (ed.), *The Universal Jewish Encyclopedia*, The Universal Jewish Encyclopedia, Inc., New York, 1943, p. 668.

Leslau, Wolf (trans.), *Falasha Anthology*, Yale University Press, New Haven, Conn., 1951, pp. 28, 33, 217, 282–3, 460.

ZIPPORAH

Asimov, Isaac, *Asimov's Guide to the Bible*, Doubleday & Co., New York, 1968, pp. 129, 168.

Berman, Colette, and Miller, Yosef, *The Beautiful People of the Book: A Tribute to Ethiopian Jews in Israel*, Millhouse Publishers, Jerusalem/New York, 1988, pp. 43, 76, 91, 109, 110, 146.

Garber, Zev, 'Jethro, Father-in-Law of Moses: Summary of Biblical and Rabbinical Material', *Forum: 50*, no. 49.

Hertz, Dr J. H. (ed.), *The Pentateuch and Haftorahs*, The Soncino Press, London, 1966, commentaries: Exodus 2: 15–22, 4: 18–26, 18: 1–10; Numbers 12: 1.

The Holy Scriptures, The Jewish Publication Society of America, Philadelphia, 1955, Exodus 2: 15, 18: 1, 18: 24, Numbers 12: 1.

The Jewish Encyclopedia, 12 vols, KTAV Publishing House, New York, 1901: vol. 4, pp. 394–5; vol. 12, pp. 686–7.

Leslau, Wolf (trans.), *Falasha Anthology*, Yale University Press, New Haven, Conn., 1951, pp. xvii–xviii, 104–5.

Sarna, Nahum M., *Exploring Exodus: The Heritage of Biblical Israel*, Schocken Books, New York, 1986, pp. 126–7.

Silver, Daniel Jeremy, *Images of Moses*, Basic Book Publishers, New York, 1982, pp. 8–9, 204–5, 291.

Wilson, Ian, *Exodus: The True Story Behind the Biblical Account*, Harper & Row Publishers, San Francisco, 1985, pp. 126, 147.

DAUGHTERS OF ZELOPHEHAD

Bialik, Hayim Naham, and Ravnitzky, Yehoshua Hanna (eds.), *The Book of Legends*, The Soncino Press, New York, 1992, p. 98.

Hertz, Dr J. H. (ed.), *The Pentateuch and Haftorahs*, The Soncino Press, London, 1966, pp. 532, 691–2, 723–4.

The Holy Scriptures, The Jewish Publication Society of America, Philadelphia, 1955, pp. 219–20, 311–12.

The Jewish Encyclopedia, 12 vols, KTAV Publishing House, New York, 1901, vol. 12, p. 655.

RUTH

Bialik, Hayim Naham (ed.), *The Book of Legends — Legends from Talmud and Midrash*, Schocken Books, New York, 1992.

Cohen, Mortimer J., *Pathways through the Bible*, second edition, The Jewish Publication Society, Philadelphia, 1960–65.

The Jewish Encyclopedia, 12 vols, KTAV Publishing House, New York, 1901, vol. 10, pp. 576–8.

Zlotowitz, Rabbi Meir, *The Book of Ruth*, Mesorah Publications, Brooklyn, New York, 1976.

ABIGAIL

Cohen, Mortimer J., *Pathways through the Bible*, second edition, The Jewish Publication Society of America, Philadelphia, 1960–65, pp. 236–8.

Goldman, S. (ed.), *Samuel*, The Soncino Books of the Bible, edited by Rabbi Dr A. Cohen, The Soncino Press, London, 1987, pp. 1–42, II Samuel 17.

The Holy Scriptures, The Jewish Publication Society of America, Philadelphia, 1961, pp. 396–9, I Samuel 25: 1–42.

The Jewish Encyclopedia, 12 vols, KTAV Publishing Co., New York, vol. 1, pp. 57–8.

Lockyer, Herbert, *All the Women of the Bible*, Zondervan Publishing House, Grand Rapids, 1967, pp. 23–5.

HULDAH

Bryant, David, *Wheels and Looms*, B. T. Batsford, London, 1987, pp. 116–118.

Encyclopedia Judaica, Macmillan Co., New York, 1971, vol. 10, pp. 1026–7, II Kings 22: 14–20.

Friedman, Richard Elliott, *Who Wrote the Bible?*, Harper & Row, New York, 1987, pp. 96–104.

Ginzberg, Louis, *Legends of the Bible*, The Jewish Publication Society of America, Philadelphia, 1909, p. 623.

Hertz, Dr J. H. (ed.), *The Pentateuch and Haftorahs*, The Soncino Press, London, 1966, pp. 937–8.

The Holy Scriptures, The Jewish Publication Society of America, Philadelphia, 1961, pp. 525–7, II Kings 22: 1–20, 23: 1–3.

The Jewish Encyclopedia, 12 vols, KTAV Publishing House, New York, 1901, vol. 6, pp. 488–9.

Slotki, I. W. (ed.), *Kings*, The Soncino Books of the Bible, edited by Rabbi Dr A. Cohen, The Soncino Press, London, 1990, pp. 300–302.

JUDITH

The Apocrypha, revised edition, Thomas Nelson & Sons, New York, 1957.

Eerdman, William, *Great Women of the Bible in Art and Literature*, William Eerdman Publishing Co., Grand Rapids, 1994, pp. 206–19.

Encyclopaedia Judaica, Keter Publishing House, Jerusalem, 1920, vol. 10.

Freedman, David Noel (ed.), *The Anchor Bible Dictionary*, Doubleday Publishers, New York, 1992, pp. 117–124.

Komroff, Manuel (ed.), *The Apocrypha*, Tudor Publication Co., New York, 1936.

Torrey, Charles Cutler, *The Apocryphal Literature*, Yale University Press, New Haven, Conn., 1945.

ESTHER

Cohen, Mortimer J., *Pathways through the Bible*, second edition, The Jewish Publication Society of America, Philadelphia, 1960–65.

Culi, Rabbi Yaakov, *The Book of Esther*, translated by Rabbi Aryeh Kaplan, Maznaim Publishing Corporation, New York, 1978.

Ginzberg, Louis, *Legends of the Bible*, The Jewish Publication Society of America, Philadelphia, 1909.

The Jewish Encyclopedia, 12 vols, KTAV Publishing House, New York, 1901, vol. 5, pp. 232–41.

GLOSSARY

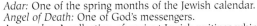

Adar: One of the spring months of the Jewish calendar.

Angel of Death: One of God's messengers.

Apocrypha: A collection of ancient Jewish writings which are not part of the Bible.

Ark: The box in which the Israelites carried the Commandments, carved on two stone tablets.

Assyria: An ancient empire which fought against the Israelites.

Bar Mitzvah: Ceremony in which a Jewish boy is accepted as a man at the age of 13.

Bat Mitzvah: Ceremony in which a Jewish girl is accepted as a woman at the age of 12 or 13.

Bible: The Torah, Writings and Prophets. Often called the 'Old Testament' by Christian writers.

Catholicism: A part of the Christian church under the authority of the Pope.

Circumcision: An operation performed on Jewish boys when they are eight days old, in which a piece of skin is removed from the penis. It does hurt, but it does not do them any harm.

Commandment: A law given by God or decreed by religious authorities.

Dead Sea Scrolls: A collection of ancient scrolls, discovered in 1948.

Fifty chiefs: The senior members of the twelve tribes of Israel.

Haggadah: Book of prayers and stories telling how the Israelites left Egypt, read at the Passover Seder.

Hamantaschen: Triangular biscuits eaten at Purim. Said to be in the shape of Haman's hat.

Hebrew: The language of ancient Israel. The Bible and most Jewish prayers are written in Hebrew.

High Priest: The senior priest of the Jews in ancient times.

Holy of Holies: The most sacred part of the Temple, where the Ark was kept. Only the High Priest was allowed to enter here, once a year, to ask God to forgive the sins of the Israelites.

House of David: The royal family of King David.

Intermarriage: Marriage between a couple with different religions.

Israelite: A member of the Jewish people.

Jerusalem: The capital of Israel.

Judaism: The Jewish religion.

Judah/Judea: Part of the ancient land of Israel.

King David: The second king of Israel.

King Josiah: A king of ancient Israel who was also a very learned and religious man.

King Saul: The first king of ancient Israel.

King Solomon: The son of King David and Bathsheba, the third king of ancient Israel.

Law: The Torah — according to the Bible, these are the laws given to Moses by God.

Matzah: Unleavened bread eaten at Passover.

Midrash: A collection of stories told by Jews to explain stories in the Bible.

Mitzvah, pl. Mitzvot: Originally 'commandments of God'; in modern times, 'good deeds'.

Moab: A country next to the ancient land of Israel.

Moabites: The people of Moab.

Mount Nebo: A mountain in the desert on the edge of the land of Israel. Moses died and was buried there.

Mount Sinai: A mountain in the Sinai desert where Moses met God and received the Commandments.

Nazi: A member of the political party which ran Germany during the Second World War. The Nazis hated the Jews and devised a plan to exterminate them.

Nebuchadnezzar: A king of the empire of Babylon. He conquered Israel and took the Jews into exile.

Passover/Pesach: The festival commemorating the Israelites' escape from Egypt.

Persia: An ancient empire including what is now Iran and Iraq.

Philistines: A tribe of people who lived in and near the ancient land of Israel.

Pogrom: A Russian word meaning an organised massacre of helpless people, often referring specifically to Jews.

Promised Land: The land which the Israelites inhabited. The Bible says that God promised this land to the first Jewish family.

Prophet: A man or woman who receives messages from God to pass on to others.

Purim: The festival commemorating the time when Queen Esther saved the Jews of Persia.

Rabbi: A Jewish teacher.

Sabbath: Saturday, a day of rest on which Jewish people are commanded not to work.

Sackcloth and ashes: A sign that someone is in mourning for a relative who has died, or that they are asking God for forgiveness.

Scribe: A kind of secretary for a king, who wrote down what happened and what the king had said. They would have had very neat handwriting!

Seder: The meal and ceremony held by Jewish families at Passover.

Succah, pl. Succot: A shack built by the Israelites on their journey through the desert. Succot are built by Jews today to remember this. When the Israelites settled in the land of Israel and had farms, families would have lived in a Succah near their fields during the harvest, to save them from going all the way home every night.

Talmud: A book written by Rabbis explaining and interpreting the laws in the Torah.

Tearing clothes: A sign of sadness. Jews will tear an item of clothing when a member of their family dies.

Temple: The Temple was built in Jerusalem by King Solomon. It was the centre for Jewish worship while the Jews lived in the land of Israel.

Ten Commandments: The first Commandments given to Moses by God.

Tent of Meeting: When the Israelites were travelling from Egypt to the land of Israel, they kept the Torah in a box and kept the box in a tent called the Tent of Meeting. This was also where the senior people from all of the tribes would meet to discuss important matters.

Torah: The first five books of the Bible, also called the Five Books of Moses. The Torah contains the early history and laws of the Jewish people. It is written on a scroll decorated with silver ornaments. 'Torah' means 'teaching' in Hebrew.

Tribe of Levi: One of the twelve tribes of Israel; Miriam, Moses and Aaron belonged to the tribe of Levi. Jewish priests were also chosen from that tribe.